HOW TO REMEMBER NAMES AND FACES

How to Develop a Good Memory

BY

ROBERT H. NUTT

1943

SIMON AND SCHUSTER · NEW YORK

Tenth Printing, January, 1947

MANUFACTURED IN THE UNITED STATES OF AMERICA
BY H. WOLFF, NEW YORK

To
Betty, Bobby, and Billy Nutt

TABLE OF CONTENTS

PART 1

THE MENTAL FILING SYSTEM

PART II

HOW TO REMEMBER NAMES AND FACES

PART ONE

THE MENTAL FILING SYSTEM

CHAPTER ONE

THE SECRET OF
A MENTAL FILING SYSTEM
THAT REALLY WORKS

YOU WERE NOT *born* with a poor memory. Remembering is a process that must be learned, just like walking, talking, eating, telling colors apart, distinguishing sounds, and telling time. You learned these when you were a child, and now you can perform them without effort, without being conscious of the mental processes involved. You can learn the process of using your memory just as thoroughly, and when you do you will have in your power a hundred times the knowledge and experience you actually put to use now.

Anyone can do it. If you want to make your experiences stick, in order to help you make later decisions and meet later problems, and if you hate the waste of relearning what you have forgotten, it will be worth your while to develop a good memory.

This book will show you how, for it is simply a logical,

tested plan for training you to index your memory scientifi-
cally, much along the lines of a filing system. I call it *The
Mental Filing System.*

There is nothing new in the idea of a memory system; men
have been developing methods of remembering since the days
of Cicero. I have based my method on the fundamental principles laid down by these earlier systems, modifying them by
the practical application of twenty years of actual teaching and
use. You can start using it immediately, applying it to everyday situations.

Why do you forget? The reason for most of the annoying
instances of forgetting is that you do not take the trouble to
connect new information with some fact you already know.
Isolated facts drop out of the mind quickly, but if you file new
knowledge in relation to something already established in your
mind, you will retain it and be able to refer to it whenever you
need it. It is simply a matter of making a special use of your
power of association, which is the beginning of all learning
processes. William James said, "In mental terms, the more
other facts a fact is associated with in the mind, the better
possession of it our memory retains. Each of its associates becomes a hook to which it hangs, a means to fish it up by when
sunk beneath the surface." Association is making *mental hooks*
from which you may fish facts out of your mind as you require
them. This Mental Filing System will provide the mental hooks
upon which to hang, or file, anything you want to remember.

Certain selected words, called KEY WORDS, are the mental hooks in your filing system. Each one represents a vivid image. Here is the system. Try it for yourself.

CHAPTER TWO

HOW TO GET
YOUR FIRST FIVE
MENTAL HOOKS

KEY WORD NUMBER ONE

1. ALARM CLOCK. Now visualize an alarm clock. This alarm clock is very large. Both hands point to the figure *1*. I tell you this not only because I want the picture to be clear, but because you are to associate it with the *number one*. *Alarm clock* is our *first* key word. To strengthen the association, remember, for example, that the alarm clock is the *first* thing you see in the morning, and it cost you *one* dollar. It rings *once* before you reach out and turn it off. ONE is ALARM CLOCK.

Take all the time you need to form these mental images. They are the basis of a memory system you will use for the rest of your life and are as vital to it as the alphabet is to your reading. If the picture vanishes or is blurred and indistinct, wait until it appears as vivid as a real picture in an advertisement.

KEY WORD NUMBER TWO

2. TROUSERS.   Go through the same process in visualizing *trousers* as you did with *alarm clock*, this time, of course, associating *trousers* with the figure 2. These *two*-legged trousers cost you *two* dollars. *Two* pair of trousers came with your suit. TWO is TROUSERS.

KEY WORD NUMBER THREE

3. CHAIR.   See the *chair* in your mind, and at the same time tie it up with the figure *3*. Think of the *chair* as having *three* parts—the back, the seat, and the legs. It's a *three*-legged chair. There is a big price tag, reading $3, tied to this *chair*. Close your eyes now and see the *chair* with its *three* parts. THREE is CHAIR.

KEY WORD NUMBER FOUR

4. TABLE.   Visualize a *four*-legged. *four*-sided table. It is set for *four* people. *Four* dollars is what you paid for this table for *four*. FOUR is TABLE.

KEY WORD NUMBER FIVE

5. NEWSPAPER.   This *newspaper* is a *Five-Star Final*. It costs *five* cents, and you read it for *five* minutes. It is a *5* o'clock edition which you bought after knocking off work at *5* o'clock. FIVE is NEWSPAPER.

These are the first five key words, and for the time being we will devote our attention to learning them thoroughly. After a few pages of practice and drill in these we will go on to higher numbers. But even before you reach these higher numbers you will find these first five helping you remember countless items you used to forget.

By this time, you are probably asking a very natural question: Why do we use just these particular key words, instead of just any five that come to mind? The answer is simply that these key words are the result of long experimentation in memory training. They have proved easy to remember, and moreover they lend themselves to a natural sequence. What is this sequence?

ONE, TWO, THREE, FOUR, FIVE

First thing in the morning, your *alarm clock* goes off.
Second, you put on your *trousers*.
Third, you sit down in a *chair*.
Fourth, you draw it up to the *table*.
Fifth, you read your *newspaper*.

The average man performs these five simple acts day in, day out, throughout his lifetime. Just because these acts are so common and so easy to remember, they form the first five key words of our Mental Filing System.

Knowing these words and seeing these images in their natural sequences is a great help, but you must also be able to shuffle them around. Get your pencil now, and test yourself with the following drill. Keep at it until you get each word correct without hesitating. Remember: *always see the image.*

Fill in each space with the proper key word:

4. . . . .   5. . . . .

1. . . . .   3. . . . .

                    2. . . . .

Did you find, in doing this test, that some one image did not come as quickly as the others? Here is a tip. Try to exaggerate the image. Try to see it bigger, brighter, and more detailed. The noted journalist, Elbert Hubbard, said the first rule of writing was "Paint the picture large." He knew that exaggeration helps the imagination and makes details stand out commandingly in the reader's mind. You will find this rule of immense value in forming your mental images. So every time you find yourself stumbling over a particular key word, stop, concentrate again on the image, and see it larger and in more brilliant colors. Don't go ahead until this weaker picture grows just as strong as the others. This should take only a minute of concentration. When you are ready, try this exercise:

Write the proper numbers against the key words:

CHAIR is No. . . . .   ALARM CLOCK is No. . . . . .

NEWSPAPER is No. . . . .   TABLE is No. . . . .

TROUSERS is No. . . . .

Read this book as a textbook. Try out each test from a practical standpoint, then proceed with your next lesson and test.

LET'S START FIRST
WITH SOMETHING SIMPLE

THOUGH YOU may not have realized it, you have already learned the fundamental principle of our memory system. You are now ready to put it to work. The first five key words are ready in your mind to help you remember something else entirely. Let us start with something fairly simple—say, the five biggest cities in the world.

In order of size, the five biggest cities are London, New York, Tokyo, Berlin, Moscow. Filing each one on its proper hook, we get:

1. Alarm clock—London
2. Trousers—New York
3. Chair—Tokyo
4. Table—Berlin
5. Newspaper—Moscow

Our object is to associate each of these cities vividly with its key word and therefore with its number. Let me explain at once that the following associations are offered merely as suggestions, to help you get started in forming your own mental images. If some other picture occurs to you which you feel is a stronger association, don't hesitate to use it. Every mind is different, and the best association is the one that works best for you.

1. *London* (alarm clock).   Towering over *London* is the biggest *clock* in the world, Big Ben. Picture yourself climbing up the tower in order to wind up the *clock* for the night, setting the hands to *one* o'clock. The word *London* is written across the dial of the clock in Old English letters. London —alarm clock.

2. *New York* (trousers).   How are you going to associate *New York* with *trousers?* Well, you bought your *new* trousers in *New* York. The *trousers* are made in *New York* by a *New York* tailor. (Although in general it is better to try to associate the item to be remembered with the key word rather than the number, in this case you can further strengthen the image by remembering that *New York* is *two* words.) New York—trousers.

3. *Tokyo* (chair).   See a Japanese in a *toque* sitting on the *chair*. His big *toe* is stuck in the neck of a bottle of *Tokay* wine, and he is yelling, "Oh, my *toe!* It's in the *Tokay*—

oh!" His toe is cut off and lying on the chair, but his *toe* is *OK*. Tokyo—chair.

4. *Berlin* (table). A group of *burly Germans* are sitting about a large *German table,* with a swastika painted on it. They are drinking *German* beer and singing songs written by Irving *Berlin.* Berlin—table.

5. *Moscow* (newspaper). Your *newspaper,* the Five-Star Final, is covered with *moss,* and a *cow* is lying on top of it, chewing at the *moss* and eating up the *paper.* This is a *moss-cow.* The headline on the *newspaper* reads FIVE-YEAR PLAN FOR MOSCOW. Moscow—newspaper.

Reread these associations, adding to them any details that make the images more vivid. Then reach for your pencil and fill in the following spaces.

Third city is............

Second city is...........

Fifth city is.............

First city is.............

Fourth city is............

If you hesitated over any of the cities, go back and concentrate on that image until the picture is perfectly clear in your mind. When pictures tend to elude you, it is because they are not sharp and definite enough.

The picture of yourself setting the hands of Big Ben and the *moss-cow* pun on Moscow must have seemed pretty ridiculous when you came across them. But as I have pointed out, exaggeration will help you remember the images. The sillier the better. If you happened to be looking out of your window and saw a man playing a harmonica while he balanced an egg on the tip of his nose, you would never forget the picture. The more ludicrous, gruesome, or farfetched a picture is, the longer it will stay in your mind, and the easier it will be for you to recall it.

This fact is most important to advertisers. They often take shrewd advantage of it to capture your attention and interest. Don't you have vivid associations of Sinclair Oil with a picture of a hideous prehistoric monster, of the insecticide Flit, with Dr. Seuss' drawings of fabulous mosquitoes fleeing from the menace of the Flit gun, and of the Chesapeake Railroad with a kitten sleeping cozily in a comfortable sleeping-car berth? All of these pictures are highly improbable and exaggerated, and in this lies their very appeal to your memory.

Now test yourself again to see how thoroughly you know the five largest cities. This time, write the number against the name of the city.

MOSCOW is No..........

NEW YORK is No.........

BERLIN is No. ....

LONDON is No...........

TOKYO is No............

It was decidedly faster this time, wasn't it?

CHAPTER FOUR

MAKING YOUR
OWN MENTAL IMAGES

IN THE LAST CHAPTER, we spoke of the importance of exaggeration in remembering an image. Another factor is *action*.

Why are actors so furious when some minor character steals a scene by the simple device of walking across the stage? Because it is an old truism in the theater that the eyes of the audience are always attracted and held by a *moving* object. In the same way, your mental images will be more vivid to you if you can put some action into them.

The more violent the action, the more attention it will get. You never forget an accident, especially a bloody one. The smallest details of the picture remain in your mind for years. For this reason, gruesome, even terrifying images make a deep impression on the mind, and should be used as much as possible.

To show how you can put action into these mental images, let us memorize another list of five items. Even though you feel you already know the first five key words thoroughly, this practice will help you.

In this list we turn from geography to death. Here is a list of the five principal causes of death in the United States, in order:

1. Heart disease

2. Cancer

3. Apoplexy

4. Pneumonia

5. Accidents

1. HEART DISEASE.   The *alarm clock* ticks like the *heart*. A red valentine heart hung over the alarm clock. *Heart trouble—alarm clock.*

2. CANCER.   *Cancer* is eating up the trousers. Cancellation marks on the *trousers. Cancer—trousers.*

3. APOPLEXY.   *Apples* are mashed on the *chair*. See the apples mashed all over the chair; the juice from the apples is running down the legs of the chair. *Apoplexy—chair.*

4. PNEUMONIA.   Someone is lying on the *table* and can barely breathe on account of *pneumonia. New-mown* hay is scattered all over the table. You pour *ammonia* over the person on the table. *Pneumonia—table.*

5. ACCIDENTS.   Big headlines in the *newspaper* with a picture of a big wreck. Five people killed. Maybe you see blood on the newspaper from the *accident*. *Accidents—newspaper*.

Read these associations carefully again. Now fill in the spaces below with the causes of death:

        2. ....

        5. ....

        3. ....

        1. .. . .

        4. ....

By this time you are probably asking a question that often puzzles my students. "If I use the same key word over and again, won't I get mixed up? Won't the pictures from one list pop in another list where they don't belong?"

Actual practice shows that this doesn't happen. The very fact that it doesn't shows what a wonderfully sensitive and obliging instrument the mind is. When you name your five largest cities, you are thinking *cities*, and the city associations pop up like figures on a cash register. You will never confuse the associations for cities with the associations for these causes of death, provided you are thinking of what you are doing and have formed vivid pictures in the first place.

Better check yourself again on the list of five principal causes of death in the United States, this time filling in the key number opposite the cause of death:

APOPLEXY is No.............

HEART DISEASE is No.............

ACCIDENTS is No.............

PNEUMONIA is No.. . ...

CANCER is No.............

CHAPTER FIVE

HOW TO REMEMBER
WHAT YOU READ

A YOUNG COLLEGE STUDENT I know, facing an exam in physics, sat up cramming the whole night before the test. By dawn he had mastered one hundred and fifty definitions simply by repeating them over and over until he "had" them. When I met him on the street a week later, I asked him how he had made out. He laughed. "Oh, I passed with flying colors. But if you asked me for one of those definitions now, I couldn't tell you, if my life depended on it!"

This is a common example of the misuse of the process of repetition in remembering. If this student had set himself the task of learning just five new definitions a day, and had repeated them once every day for a week, and then once each week for a month, he would have injected his hundred and fifty definitions into his brain gently, painlessly, and *permanently*. Every educator knows that cramming a head with knowledge is like loading a cannon. The powder is good for one blast, at examination. and then disappears into air.

The secret of learning by repetition is to repeat at intervals.

31

That is why I have given you only five key words to remember so far. You might call this the first lesson. Tonight, before you go to sleep, review the five key images—*alarm clock, trousers, chair, table,* and *newspaper*—in your mind slowly, seeing them clearly. Then do the same with the list of the five largest cities.

In the morning, when you wake up and see the alarm clock, run through the lists again. You can do this while you are dressing. Notice, I do not ask you to take time away from your work to improve your memory. Any remnant of spare time will do—while you are shaving or having your shoes shined. If you are a housewife, you might try it while you are washing the dishes or making the beds.

In the beginning you can't go over these lists too frequently. Merely reading a memory system is not mastering it, for no power on earth can make you remember things that you have never learned. So take your time—as much time as you please. No one is going to try to outdistance you. If you go slowly, learning the key words thoroughly, I promise you this memory system will enable you to remember practically anything you want to remember.

One way to find out if you have mastered the material presented so far is to try your hand at a stiff speed drill. The following is a skip-about test, included for the practical purpose of giving you practice in pulling out of your lists the *one* answer you want.

It is doubtful that you will ever be called upon suddenly to name the five largest cities in the world or the five principal

causes of death in the United States, any more than you are
regularly called upon to recite the entire alphabet. But although
you may never have to give a complete list, you may at some
time want to know a single fact, such as what the second cause
of death in the United States is or which is the fourth largest
city in the world. This test will help you develop speed and
ease in picking facts out of your mental file.

Place a clock where you can check the time easily, and
keep a record of your speed. See if you can finish this drill in
three minutes.

SPEED DRILL

What is the *second* largest city? ....

What is the *third* cause of death in the United States?.......

What is Key Word Number *Two?* ....

What is the *fifth* largest city? ....

What is the *fourth* cause of death?......................

What is the largest city? ....

What is Key Word Number *Four?*..... ....

What is the *second* cause of death?......................

What is Key Word Number *One?* ....

What is the *third* largest city? ....

What is the *first* cause of death?........................

What is Key Word Number *Five?* ....

What is the *fifth* cause of death?........................

What is the *fourth* largest city? ....

What is Key Word Number *Three?* ....

Time.... ....

CHAPTER SIX

FIVE MORE KEYS
THAT UNLOCK
MEMORY

Do YOU BEGIN to realize what magic lies in these key words? You now have five keys to unlock chambers of your memory swiftly and surely. Naturally, with *ten* key words you can double the storage room. Let's have a look at the next five, and see how much more easily the mental images come after the practice of the previous chapters.

KEY WORD NUMBER SIX

6. AUTOMOBILE. This is easy to remember. The *automobile* is a *six*-cylinder car, and the license plate has *six* figures, all *sixes*—666,666. It seats *six* persons and *six* payments are still due on it. SIX is AUTOMOBILE.

KEY WORD NUMBER SEVEN

7. POLICEMAN. He is *seven* feet tall and *seven* feet around, this big *policeman*. His badge number is *seven*.

With his arm outstretched for you to stop, he looks like a figure 7. SEVEN is POLICEMAN.

KEY WORD NUMBER EIGHT

8. REVOLVING DOOR.   Think of a pair of *revolving doors.* When they swing around, what kind of a figure do they make? That's right—a figure *8,* laid on its side. These *revolving doors* are in front of a restaurant in which you *ate.* As you pushed the *revolving door* you heard the clock striking *eight.* EIGHT is REVOLVING DOOR.

KEY WORD NUMBER NINE

9. MAILBOX.   When you see a government mailbox in pro-file, it looks like a figure *9.* The number on this mailbox is 999. The next collection is at *nine* o'clock. NINE is MAIL-BOX.

KEY WORD NUMBER TEN

10. GENERAL-DELIVERY WINDOW.   This general-de-livery window has *ten* bars. Every time you go to the *general-delivery window ten* fingers reach out to collect your *ten*-dollar bill. The shelf under the *general-delivery* *window* is made of *tin* and needs attention. TEN is GEN-ERAL-DELIVERY WINDOW.

These second five key words follow upon each other in a natural sequence of action, just as the first five did. After you have finished reading your *newspaper*, which was *five*, you...

6. get into your *automobile*,
7. are stopped by a *policeman*,
8. walk through a *revolving door*,
9. go to the *mailbox*,
10. and call at the *general-delivery window*.

Turn back now and study these second five key words until you know them just as well as the first five. Go through them again and again. Say them backwards and forwards. When you feel sure of yourself, try the following exercise:

Write the key word against the key number:

9. ....   10. ....

5. ....   7. ....

8. ....   3. ....

1. ....   2. ....

4. ....   6. ....

Now, just to make sure, write the key numbers against the key words:

AUTOMOBILE is No....   POLICEMAN is No....

TROUSERS is No....   CHAIR is No....

GENERAL-DELIVERY WINDOW   REVOLVING DOOR is No....

   is No....   TABLE is No....

NEWSPAPER is No....   ALARM CLOCK is No....

MAILBOX is No....

CHAPTER SEVEN

WHAT MUST I REMEMBER TO DO TODAY ?

WHETHER WE ARE lawyers, surgeons, salesmen, housewives, symphonic or streetcar conductors, there is one kind of remembering that is necessary to all of us. It is right here that most of us commit our major sins. We all, no matter what our business or financial status is, must remind ourselves to do numerous things from day to day. We may forget to mail letters, to make train reservations, to bring home sun-tan lotion when our wives are leaving for the country. Frequently these oversights get us into consequences ridiculously out of proportion to their importance.

For some reason or other, when *we* forget, it always seems a most natural and human failing, but when other people forget, we harbor in our hearts the conviction that they did it out of sheer indifference or downright contrary cussedness.

Show me the household where the temperature doesn't shoot down to zero under this kind of barrage: "Did you send my suit to the cleaners? Did you call the landlord to fix the sink? Why haven't you paid the gas bill?"

You don't need a secretary to remind you of the little things you might forget. Even a secretary's memory is not infallible. You can, however, remember petty details independently and surely with the ten key words you already know. Make your own Mental Memorandum List.

You don't need any fixed time for filing your memoranda on your mental hooks, as you do when you make memoranda in your little notebook. You merely file them in order as you think of them. In the act of running for a streetcar, you may remember that as soon as you get to the office you must look over the report of yesterday's meeting. Very well, file that idea at once on *alarm clock*, key word number one.

You may be buying cigars when you recall that sometime during the day you must telephone Schmidt and Company about their bill. File this idea on *trousers*, key word number two. And so on, filing each memorandum *in order* on its proper mental hook.

Here is a memorandum list of ten "musts" drawn up and carried out by one of my students. Of course, you will want to make out your own personal list, but an examination of his will help you get the idea.

1. Buy a can of green paint.

2. Get the car greased.

3. Buy a hat.

4. Pay fire insurance.

5. Feed the dog.

6. Order coal.

7. Exchange shirts.

8. Get bicycle for Junior.

9. Send flowers to my wife.

10. Reserve tennis court.

had to remember to

to paint that trellis.
ith green paint drip-
pouring a bucket of
n clock—Buy can of

get the car greased.
with grease, after I
ockets are filled with
greased.

3. This hat is a disgrace. I need a new one. Let's see—I want to sit on the chair, but the seat of the chair is piled high with hats, and hats are hanging all over the back of the chair. I sit down hard on a straw hat and crush it on the chair. *Chair—Buy a hat.*

4. Another notice this morning to pay my fire insurance. See my table going up in flames, with my policy in the middle of it. I burn my hands trying to snatch the fire-insurance policy off the table. *Table—Pay fire insurance.*

5. Feed the dog. I always forget this, but Bozo doesn't. See Bozo chewing up my newspaper because he's so hungry. The dog is lying on the newspaper, eating the raw, bloody meat. See dog food smeared all over the newspaper. *Newspaper—Feed the dog.*

6. I'd better get the winter's coal in early this year and avoid delay. See the automobile filled with coal, in a fog of coal dust. I have to shovel out all the coal before I can get into the automobile. I open the auto door and coal rushes out, and I can't see the road because the windshield is black with coal dust. *Automobile—Order coal.*

7. My wife always buys my shirts too large. See a policeman in shirt tails stopping traffic to come over to me. He takes off his shirt, I take off mine, and we exchange shirts. *Policeman—Exchange shirts.*

8. I told Junior I'd buy him a bike if he kept the yard clean. See Junior riding around and around in a revolving door on his new bike. He's getting dizzier and dizzier and finally falls off his bike. The revolving door whirls the crushed

bike and bleeding boy swiftly around. *Revolving door— Get bicycle for Junior.*

9. Tomorrow's our anniversary and I mustn't forget to send flowers to my wife. You know how women are. See bright red flowers growing out of the mailbox on the corner, and water and earth running down its sides. I reach into the mailbox slot to pick the flowers and am stuck sharply by thorns. *Mailbox—Send flowers to my wife.*

10. Oscar is coming out this week end for tennis (good old Oscar!) *Tennis* is the *tenth* thing to remember. Ten tennis rackets are hanging on the bars of the window. You are throwing ten tennis balls at the man in the window. Some of the tennis balls get stuck between the bars of the window. You break the glass in the general-delivery window with a tennis ball. *General-delivery window— Reserve tennis court.*

You might want to see how many of the items you can now recall. However, I'm not asking you to check yourself on this list. It was included to show you how a real person was able to use the Mental Filing System to remember ten things he had to do on a particular day. Now that you see how he filed his memorandum list, I suggest you make one of your own. Fill out the following spaces with a number of things *you* want to remember to do tomorrow. Here is your chance to gather up some loose ends that you have been forgetting. It will, as well, enable you to get started using this system in your own everyday affairs.

THINGS I AM GOING TO DO TOMORROW

(Hook them up with the key words)

1. ALARM CLOCK . . . .
2. TROUSERS . . . .
3. CHAIR . . . .
4. TABLE . . . .
5. NEWSPAPER . . . .
6. AUTOMOBILE . . . .
7. POLICEMAN . . . .
8. REVOLVING DOOR . . . .
9. MAILBOX . . . .
10. GENERAL-DELIVERY WINDOW . . . .

Review this list carefully, building up a vivid, colorful, and definite mental image for each item. Always make the key word the basis for your picture.

Now cover the list and see if you can write it below without hesitation. This test is jumbled simply to test whether or not your key words form an important part of the images. I have often found that people forget because the key-word image is too loosely associated. Naturally, when you come to use your list, you will refer to the items in regular order, not as they will appear below.

10. . . . .   9. . . . .

 5. . . . .   6. . . . .

 2.   4. . . . .

 7.   8. . . . .

 1. . . . .   3. . . . .

If you filled out the test above quickly and without hesitating, your mental images are excellent. Tomorrow you are actually going to do all these things from memory. To fasten them securely in your mind, run over the associations once more after you get into bed tonight.

CHAPTER EIGHT

HOW WILL I *REMEMBER* TO REMEMBER?

BUT, YOU WILL SAY, how am I going to remember in the morn-ing that I have a memory system, that I have filed a memoran-dum list, and that I am going to do all these things today? In short, how will I remember to remember?

Here is where our first key word serves a double purpose, for few of us are fortunate enough not to have to awaken in the morning to the overture of an *alarm clock*. Even if the alarm is not set, your first conscious act is to glance at the dial to see what time it is.

Even then, you rarely jump out of bed immediately. You stretch, scratch, yawn—and begin to remember. This is the simplest, most favorable time to review your plans for the day. But if it doesn't work for you, you will find any other regular daily act useful for the purpose.

Businessmen, I find, usually like to review their lists the

first thing upon arriving at the office. One executive, who attended my classes and uses the system constantly to remember the endless details of a large publishing business, makes it a habit to run through his list each morning when he takes off his hat and hangs it on the hat tree. Another does it in the subway, a third in the elevator on his ride to the twenty-second floor.

Choose whatever time is most convenient for you, but make it the time of some definite act you perform regularly, so that it will become a fixed habit.

Some people "unhook" their files as soon as they reach the office, writing down the list on a memorandum pad, where it can be seen. There is no reason why you shouldn't do this, if it makes you feel safer, although it isn't necessary if you check yourself several times a day to see if you are carrying out your schedule. This memory system, however, is presented for nothing more than your own convenience, so please use it in the way that best suits your own habits.

At this point I should like to answer another question students frequently ask: If key word number one on today's list means "Buy a can of green paint," and tomorrow means "Pay the telephone bill," won't I get the two confused and buy green paint both days instead of paying the bill on the second?

No. These are temporary lists, and the beauty of it is that you drop them as soon as you are through with them. Notice that these lists are only to be remembered from day to day; they are merely impressed upon the mind strongly enough to last twenty-four hours. There is no quicker way of dismissing them than to mark the items, as accomplished, "finished business," and never think of them again.

CHAPTER NINE

FIVE LITTLE WORDS
THAT INCREASE YOUR MEMORY
BY A THIRD

THE TEN KEY WORDS you already know are the ones you are going to use most. But knowing fifteen will help you still more, every day. For real efficiency, you should have this many ready for instant use. Here are key words 11 through 15.

KEY WORD NUMBER ELEVEN

11. SIDEWALK. This is easy to visualize, for the two *sidewalks* on the sides of a street form two parallel lines, just like the figure *11*. ELEVEN is SIDEWALK.

KEY WORD NUMBER TWELVE

12. ELEVATOR. See a light in the elevator, flashing the number *12* and a sign reading CAPACITY 12 PERSONS.

At *twelve* o'clock the elevator is always crowded with at least *twelve* passengers. TWELVE is ELEVATOR.

KEY WORD NUMBER THIRTEEN

13.   FLOOR.   *Thirteen* is considered an unlucky number, so many skyscrapers have no *thirteenth floor*. When you get off at the *thirteenth floor*, you step out and promptly fall on the unlucky *thirteenth floor*. THIRTEEN is FLOOR.

KEY WORD NUMBER FOURTEEN

14.   DOCTOR. What a man this *doctor* is! At the age of *fourteen* he has *fourteen* degrees, *fourteen* letters after his name. He charges you *fourteen* dollars a visit. FOURTEEN is DOCTOR.

KEY WORD NUMBER FIFTEEN

15.   BED. See an enormous bed, *fifteen* by *fifteen* feet. It's an antique bed, with the date *1500* embroidered in gold on the canopy. Louis *XV* once owned it. It cost *fifteen* hundred dollars. FIFTEEN is BED.

We can fit key words eleven, twelve, thirteen, fourteen, and fifteen into a sequence. After you leave the *general-delivery window* (10), you . . .

11. walk on the *sidewalk,*

12. enter an *elevator,*

13. get off at the thirteenth *floor,*

14. go in to see the *doctor,* who

15. sends you to *bed.*

Study these key words, adding any personal associations you can think of, until you know them as well as the first ten. When you feel you do, fill in the following test:

Write the key word against its number:

13. ....

11. ....

12. ....

15. ....

14. ....

Double-check by placing the right number against the key word:

BED ....

SIDEWALK ....

FLOOR ....

DOCTOR ....

ELEVATOR ....

If you are certain you now know these new key words as well as the old ones, prove it by the following time test. You should be able to fill all the spaces below, without the slightest hesitation, in 1 minute. Time yourself with a watch.

10. . . . .

2. . . . .

11. . . . .

6. . . . .

9. . . . .

14. . . . .

1. . . . .

8. . . . .

3. . . . .

12. . . . .

7. . . . .

15. . . . .

5. . . . .

13. . . . .

4. . . . .

How long did you take?   . . . .

At the first opportunity have a friend write down, slowly, fifteen different details for you to remember, telling you the number and detail as he writes it. You will amaze him by recalling them.

CHAPTER TEN

A SHOPPING LIST
A WOMAN CAN'T FORGET

THE WOMEN who have been reading this book have probably been waiting all along for a suggestion for a practical application of the Mental Filing System to their own activities. This chapter is dedicated to the ladies, and I hope to show them how to save extra steps and minimize exasperation by systematizing one of their daily household duties—making a shopping list.

Every day, as a woman goes about her house, she makes mental notes of things that must be ordered or replaced. A dripping faucet must be tightened, a squeaky blind repaired, a sweater mended, a new supply of soap put in. Yet at the end of a day, she has often forgotten to attend to several of these items, just because each one in itself is trivial.

Every woman wants to maintain a smoothly running household and be every bit as efficient in her job as her husband is in his. The Mental Filing System, used every day, will prove to be much more convenient and reliable than the old-fashioned "household reminders" and shopping lists. I know women who regard it as just as necessary a part of their household equipment as the kitchen range.

Take the problem of the shopping list. If you wait until just before you leave the house to shop to write down what you need, you know what usually happens. You forget some one item—usually the very one you need most. That means a second trip to the store or a frantic telephone call, possibly with a delivery charge attached to it. And every now and then, for you are only human, you arrive at the store to realize that you have left your shopping list on the kitchen table.

The use of the Mental Filing System instead of a written shopping list is the solution to your troubles. *You make up your list as you go along, and retain it in your head.* You can't leave it on the kitchen table. Errands, groceries, and all needed household supplies are filed at the very moment that you first notice a need for them. If you happen to be scrubbing the bathroom sink when you notice that there is only a thin sliver of toilet soap left, you file *soap* at once on your list of key words. You don't have to dry your hands or hunt for a pencil to do this. When the mail comes half an hour later, you remember you need stamps. You immediately hang *stamps* on its proper key word and go about your work confident that when you go to shop, everything you need will come to mind automatically, as you call up its key word.

For the sake of practice, let us take a fairly typical grocery list and see how the items, in spite of their similarity, may be filed reliably on the fifteen key words we already know.

Imagine you are planning a chicken dinner for Sunday, and you will have to get these things at the store:

1. Butter	8. Chicken
2. Eggs	9. Milk
3. Sirup	10. Bananas
4. Sugar	11. Flour
5. Strawberries	12. Coffee
6. Vinegar	13. Onions
7. Tomatoes	14. Lettuce

15. Salad dressing

1. The *butter* has melted and is running all over the *alarm clock*. You attempt to pick up the *alarm clock*, but it is so greasy with the melted *butter* that it slips out of your hand into the tub of *butter.* You are oiling the works of the *alarm clock* with *butter. Alarm clock—butter.*

2. The *eggs* are broken in your husband's *trousers* pockets. You put your hand in the *trousers* pocket and get the sticky *egg* all over your hand. Then you wipe the *egg* off on to the *trousers. Trousers—eggs.*

3. The *sirup* is running all over the *chair*. You sit down in the *chair* and the *sirup* sticks you to the seat of the *chair* so that you can't get up. *Chair—sirup.*

4. The *sugar* bowl is upset and the *sugar* is spilled all over the *table* and the flies are buzzing around it. Your family sits down to the *table* and has nothing to eat but *sugar*. *Table—sugar.*

5. *Strawberries*—ripe, red, juicy *strawberries*—are mashed all over the *newspaper*. You probably mash the *strawberries* when you pick up the *newspaper*. Your *newspaper* is *buried* in *straw*. *Newspaper—strawberries.*

6. You are pouring *vinegar* all over your *automobile*. In fact, you are washing your *automobile* in *vinegar*. You run out of gas, so you fill up the tank of the *automobile* with *vinegar*. A bottle of vinegar breaks and runs all over the seat of the car. *Automobile—vinegar.*

7. Red, juicy *tomatoes* are splattered and mashed all over the *policeman*. You realize a lifelong ambition and throw a *tomato* at the *policeman*, hitting him square on the nose. *Policeman—tomatoes.*

8. *Chickens* are in all the compartments of the *revolving door*. As you go through the *revolving door*, the *chickens*

fly up in your face. See the feathers flying in the door. Maybe you mash a *chicken* in the *revolving door* and it bleeds all over the *revolving door*. *Revolving door— chicken.*

9. A bottle of *milk* is broken in the *mailbox* and is running out all down the sides of the *mailbox*. *Mailbox—milk.*

10. A bunch of *bananas* is hanging on the bars of the *general-delivery window*. Possibly you sit in the *general-delivery window* every morning eating a *banana*. *General-delivery window—bananas.*

11. See dozens and dozens of sacks of *flour* broken all over the *sidewalk*. *Sidewalk—flour.*

12. There is a large urn of *coffee* in the center of the *elevator* with steam arising from it. Everyone riding up in the *elevator* is drinking *coffee*. *Elevator—coffee.*

13. The *floor* is covered with *onions* and people are sitting on the *floor* peeling the *onions* and crying their eyes out. Your eyes begin to water from the *onions* as you step on to the *floor*. *Floor—onions.*

14. The *doctor* is munching on a big head of *lettuce*. He holds the *lettuce* out to you and says, "*Let us* eat more *lettuce*." *Doctor—lettuce.*

15. You want to get into *bed,* but the *bed* is overflowing with *salad dressing.* You are mixing a salad on the bed and pouring salad dressing on it. You are *dressing* when you see the *bed* covered with *salad dressing.* Bed—*salad dressing.*

At your first reading of these associations you may feel that the images are too much like one another to be easily remembered. But when you test yourself, you will find that you have no difficulty in recalling them. We want to forget this kind of list, anyway, just as soon as it has served its purpose, and I believe you will find that *one reading,* without repetition, will fix it in mind for several hours.

Without studying the associations or reading the list again, see how many of the items you can write in the spaces below:

1. . . . .

2. . . . .

3. . . . .

4. . . . .

5. . . . .

6. . . . .

7. . . . .

8. . . . .

9. . . . .

10. . . . .

11. . . . .
12. . . . .
13. . . . .
14. . . . .
15. . . .   .

CHAPTER ELEVEN

HOW SALESMEN SELL THEIR MEMORIES FOR CASH

A SALESMAN should find infinite value in the use of the Mental Filing System, for all sales points and routine can be filed with it and remembered just as easily as the shopping list in the last chapter or the list of the world's largest cities. He may know his product thoroughly, but many a sale has fallen through because the salesman was not able to present *all* the principal sales points to a potential customer.

The manufacturer of a well-known make of oil burner asked me to give a talk to his salesmen and see if I could suggest anything to improve their selling technique. I opened my talk with a question: "Can any of you tell me the ten selling points of your oil burner?" No one—not even the sales manager—could oblige. They carried all kinds of literature explaining these ten points in detail, and admitted they had tried to memorize them. Yet frequently they would forget from three to six of them when a customer confronted them. Several of the salesmen said they had lost important sales through omitting one or two points. One told me he had once called back to get an order from a man he considered sold on the oil burner only to hear, "I bought another furnace because yours didn't have the *safety* feature." The salesman protested that his product also had that feature and tried to explain it, but the prospect had already signed an order with the man who had remembered to bring it out in his sales talk.

I asked the sales manager to get his list of sales points and read them through to me once. I knew them cold in five minutes. The Mental Filing System had helped me do in that brief period what the salesmen had been unable to learn in several months.

This is the list of ten sales points about the oil burner that these men were supposed to have at their finger tips:

1. Dependable	6. Clean
2. Economical	7. Safe
3. Continuous hot water	8. Long life
4. Trouble-free	9. Compact
5. Even temperature	10. Attractive

This is how I hooked the sales points on to the key words so the salesmen could present their argument smoothly and in correct order:

1. *Dependable* (alarm clock). Nothing is more *dependable* than your *alarm clock.* You depend on your *alarm clock* to keep accurate time and you *depend* on it to go off at

the time set. Good old *dependable alarm clock*. The oil heater is as *dependable* as an *alarm clock*.

2. *Economical* (trousers). You keep all your money—all your *economic* wealth—in your *trousers* pockets. You have only one pair of *trousers* because you are *economical*, and your tailor cut them short to be *economical* with material. They are *economical trousers*.

3. *Continuous hot water* (chair). *Hot water* runs *continuously* over the *chair*. A spigot is attached to the *chair*, and the water is so *hot* the *chair* is *continuously* bathed in clouds of steam. When you sit on this *chair* you are in *continuous hot water*.

4. *Trouble-free* (table). There is no *trouble* to this *table* at all. You can take it apart and put it together without *trouble*. It's a *trouble-free table*. See a big smiling face painted on the *table* top. The *table* is *trouble-free*, just like the oil burner.

5. *Even temperature* (newspaper). The weather report in this *newspaper* says, "Tomorrow: *Even temperature*." See a thermometer lying on the *newspaper* with the mercury always at 72 degrees, an *even temperature*.

6. *Clean* (automobile). Picture a spotlessly *clean* white *automobile*. You are washing the *automobile* so *clean* that it shines. The *automobile*, like the oil burner, is *clean*.

7. *Safe* (policeman). The *policeman* is the symbol of *safety*. He is sitting on a *safe*, keeping things *safe* for you. He holds up a sign, SAFETY. Or you see the *policeman* playing baseball and he slides into home plate—he's *safe*.

8. *Long life* (revolving door). The *revolving door* is lying on its side, and it looks very *long*. Inside the *revolving door* are stacked piles of *life*-insurance policies printed with large letters LONG LIFE. The *revolving door* itself is made out of four giant-size red copies of *Life* magazine.

9. *Compact* (mailbox). Your *mailbox* is very *compact*. You open up your *mailbox* and a cloud of powder envelops you from a lady's open *compact*. Your *mailbox* is packed with *compacts*.

10. *Attractive* (general-delivery window). There are *tracks* leading up to the *general-delivery window*. The *tracks* bring you to an *attractive* girl sitting in the *general-delivery window*. You say, "1 was *attracted* to you. I followed your *tracks*." Look at her again. Doesn't she look *attractive* sitting there in the window?

Of course, knowing these ten sales points is of no practical use to you, but memorizing them in this way will be valuable practice. The fact that they are so extremely abstract will help you when you come to filing points of your own. If you are a salesman, a few minutes of applied application will fix in your mind the sales points you want to retain about that automobile, refrigerator, insurance policy, or whatever it is you are selling. So, for the sake of practice, I strongly recommend your reading over the associations I made for the oil-burner salesmen until you know them well enough to attempt the following test:

6th sales point	3rd sales point . . . .
1st sales point	2nd sales point . . . .
10th sales point	5th sales point . . . .
8th sales point	7th sales point . . . .
4th sales point	9th sales point . . . .

When you come to apply the Mental Filing System to the attributes of your particular product, make your pictures large and as unusual as you possibly can. You will be able to remember any number of items. Take your time. They are facts you can use all year long, and it will pay you dividends to go over them until you are sure of them. At the next meeting of salesmen, you will probably be the only one to surprise your sales manager by reeling off all the new sales features without an omission.

CHAPTER TWELVE

THE ART OF FORGETTING
THE RIGHT THINGS

BACK IN 1885, the German scientist Hermann Ebbinghaus made the first experimental studies in remembering and forgetting. What he discovered then still holds true today—that using the common method of memorizing, we forget forty per cent within twenty minutes and seventy-five per cent by the end of the week! Doesn't it stand to reason, then, that if you are going to bother to learn things once, you might just as well go to a little extra trouble and protect your investment of time? You can do this easily by repeating briefly what you have learned once a day for a week, and then once a week for a month.

There have been men with a genius for memory, but their feats lie entirely outside the experience of us ordinary mortals. Lord Macaulay could memorize entire books at a single reading, Mozart as a boy wrote down the score of an oratorio after hearing it once, and Dumas *père* never forgot anything he had read. This course in memory training cannot claim to teach you to duplicate such miracles. It is based simply on the laws of the workings of the minds of normal men, and its success is due to the fact that few people realize the potential powers of their thinking processes.

You and I remember only what we know, and we know only what we remember. The art I can teach you is the ability to use to the best advantage what you know, to be able to draw upon the great storehouse of your memory *when you will*—at a moment's notice. The more easily you can accomplish that seeming miracle, the farther and faster you will travel toward your ultimate success in life. And every step you are taking in these pages is a long one in that direction.

This brings us to our next important consideration: *what shall we take the trouble to remember?* We know of course that we neither can nor want to remember everything. To make our memories serve us intelligently, we have to be able to choose the things we want to remember and concentrate on developing a selective type of memory. Dr. R. S. Woodworth, of the National Research Council and Columbia University, after testing the memories of countless subjects, has come to two significant conclusions:

1. That everyone has greater power of memory than he imagines.

2. That although intensive training produces great improvement in memory, training does not develop the

general faculty of memory, but simply increases the particular kind of memory job that is practiced.

From this you will conclude that to develop your memory in order to increase your personal efficiency you must first choose the kind of remembering on which you want to concentrate. If you learn to memorize poetry effectively, your friends may consider you more cultured and you may get extra enjoyment out of life, but it will not help you to remember the grocery list. Nor will strengthening your memory for geography or history help you to remember names and faces.

To help you decide what kind of memory you yourself want to cultivate, I suggest that you get a piece of paper right now, and write across the top the business or profession in which you are now engaged. Below that write the answers to the following questions. Take your time, thinking about the answers carefully:

1. Do my activities bring me into constant contact with people?

2. Would cultivating a better memory for names and faces pay dividends in my work?

3. Does my work necessitate my knowing many facts and figures?

4. Is a general cultural background of miscellaneous information important in my work?

5. Outside of business, what specific kind of memory would I like to cultivate for my own enjoyment?

6. Based on these questions, what kind of memory should I go about developing first?

By studying your answers thoughtfully, you will have a pretty clear and definite idea of what things you should make an effort to remember, and what you can afford to forget.

A surgeon, for instance, will want to remember the bones and tissues of the body, the kinds of surgical instruments and their uses, the virtues of the drugs and medicines in his *materia medica*, the history and development of the art of healing, and most of what he has read or learned of the achievements of other medical scientists. In addition, he will want to retain enough of his nonmedical reading to hold up his head in a general conversation. If he is fortunate enough to have some outside interest, such as collecting stamps or amateur photography, he will want to develop his memory along that line too. He, like all men, will also find it advisable to remember the dates of his wedding anniversary and family birthdays, as well as personal data about his patients and colleagues.

With all this information and more to remember, wouldn't it be the height of folly for him to waste energy remembering the precise date of Congress's approval of the act authorizing the Reconstruction Finance Corporation? You agree, of course, that the chances are a thousand to one against a surgeon's ever requiring such information.

On the other hand, a lawyer, a politician, a banker, or an editorial writer might be called upon to produce such an item at a moment's notice, out of his head. Inability to do so might even appear a serious reflection on his general qualifications.

CHAPTER THIRTEEN

CASE HISTORY
OF A MEMORY
AND HOW IT GREW

AT ANY TIME at all our memory may be the very key for opening opportunities we have long been seeking. You are familiar with the common story of an unknown actor's quick rise to fame when he was able to take over the leading role the night the star suddenly fell ill. Ethel Barrymore got her first big chance when the stage manager discovered she had memorized every part in *His Excellency the Governor* and was ready to step into the leading lady's shoes at once. Toscanini, the great conductor, was "discovered" the night he substituted for another conductor on the spur of the moment. He, of all the men in the orchestra, happened to know the score of the opera by heart because his eyesight was too poor to depend upon the written score, and could mount the podium without qualms. Neither Miss Barrymore nor Toscanini was born with unusual memories—they simply made use of the mental powers they had.

Likewise, one of the most remarkable memory feats in history was performed only a few years ago by a man who started with just a normal memory, Dean Roscoe Pound of the Harvard Law School.

Roscoe Pound was in England when he was asked to deliver a series of lectures on *Interpretations of Legal History* at Cambridge University. All the references and source material from which he could take notes were in America, two thousand miles away. The subject called for constant allusion to cases, judgments, opinions, and laws, with lengthy verbatim quotations giving the exact title, chapter, page, and even paragraph numbers of the books from which they were taken. Nevertheless, Dean Pound delivered his lectures, relying entirely upon his memory.

Later, when it was possible to check a typescript of the lectures with the material he had quoted. it was found that he had made only two errors—two wrong page numbers, due to the fact that the type in the figures was blurred!

A performance like this sounds incredible, until you discover how Pound prepared himself for his career. Like Toscanini, he was cursed—or possibly blessed—with poor eyesight. When he was still a very young man, in law school, he began to fear early blindness. In spite of strong glasses and eye exercises, the little circle of visibility on the pages of his law books grew smaller and dimmer. Ahead of him he saw only a blasted career and a tragically lonely life. Then he thought if he could make his mind substitute for his eyes—if he could *remember* the important points he read, he could carry his law books in his mind, and escape the constant references to the printed page that tortured his ailing eyes.

He recalled a game he used to play with his sister, when they were children. When they read together, out of the same book, the first to finish a page would recite as much as possible of what he had just read. At first they did it just for fun, keeping each other's score, yet in a short time they had developed an amazing proficiency in remembering stories and whole books. The secret was their concentration on "getting the sense" of each page; the rest was just a matter of practice and repetition.

So when Roscoe Pound found his eyesight failing, he began to memorize his law books, becoming a living compendium of juridical knowledge. But note that even he did not attempt to remember *everything* he read.

"Early in my effort to develop a good memory," he says, "I decided it was important not to overload it with a mass of useless material. By that, I mean matter that could be of no service to me in my work and daily life, or which at the best would only be of occasional service."

So the answer to the question, "What shall we take the trouble to remember?" asked in the last chapter, is this:

Decide what kinds of facts and material are going to prove most useful to you in your professional or personal life, and concentrate on developing your memory for these.

CHAPTER FOURTEEN

HOW TO SPEAK IN PUBLIC WITHOUT NOTES

TEACHERS OF public speaking are always warning us in thunderous voices against memorizing speeches. And they are right. Did you ever listen in agony to a man reel through a talk he had spent hours committing to heart? His whole attitude notifies you at once of three things: (1) that he is scared to death of you; (2) that he will consider himself lucky to be alive and breathing at the final period; (3) that he will be overwhelmingly grateful when the whole thing is over and he can make his escape.

And you, the audience, react in a perfectly natural and human manner: you are exasperated with him, irritated and resentful that he has forced you to witness his sufferings.

Yet the chances are that when it comes your turn to make a speech, you will make the same error. You will write out your talk beforehand, learn it all by rote, and recite it out loud until it has lost all of its freshness, all of its surprise, and all of its meaning.

Why do we persist in falling into this familiar trap when

we *know* better? Simply because we are afraid of forgetting. We lie awake at night racking our souls with clammy visions of what will happen if we cannot remember the speech when we get up to deliver it. And we overlook the all-important fact that it is the *content* of the speech, *the general outline*, that we want to remember, and not the exact wording or the exact phrase.

Making a speech from a written outline, or from notes, is a little better than reciting from memory, but not much. Notes advertise the fact that you have prepared your speech in advance, and that destroys the happiest illusion with which a speaker can beguile his audience—the illusion that the entire talk is spontaneous, and has arisen as a sudden collaboration between the speaker and his listeners.

Now, naturally, talks must be prepared. You must know what you are going to say, what ideas you are going to get across, and what points you are going to cover. But the exact wording of these ideas should be left to the moment when you come face to face with your audience. What you say then may not pass the most rigid tests of grammar or oratory, but you will at least be natural, unstudied, and spontaneous. Remember, it is infinitely better to grope occasionally for a word, or to throw in a couple of "ers," than it is to be flawlessly correct and sound like a well-rehearsed phonograph record. Your audience will forgive practically anything in the world, if you are human and interesting, but they will never forgive the inexcusable crime of boring them.

But if you're not allowed to memorize your speech or read

your talk, and you're not permitted to use notes, how can you possibly mount that platform with the calm assurance that you will remember everything you wanted to say? By using your Mental Filing System and filing the *outline* of your talk on your mental hooks.

Does it work? Let me quote a passage from Dale Carnegie's book, *Public Speaking and Influencing Men in Business*, where he cites the method used by Mark Twain:

"The discovery of how to use his visual memory enabled Mark Twain to discard the notes that had hampered his speeches for years. Here is his story as he told it in *Harper's Magazine:*

" 'Thirty years ago I was delivering a memorized lecture every night, and every night I had to help myself with a page of notes to keep from getting myself mixed. The notes consisted of beginnings of sentences, and were eleven in number, and they ran something like this:

" 'In that region the weather—

" 'At that time it was a custom—

" 'But in California one never heard—

" 'Eleven of them. They initialed the brief of the lecture and protected me against skipping. But they all looked about alike on the page; they formed no picture; I had them by heart, but I could never with certainty remember the order of their succession; therefore, I always had to keep those notes by me and look at them every little while. Once I mislaid them; you will not be able to imagine the terrors of that evening. I now saw that I must invent some other protection.

So I got ten of the initial letters by heart in their proper order
—I, A, B, and so on—and I went on the platform the next
night with these marked in ink on my ten fingernails. But it
didn't answer. I kept track of the fingers for a while; then I
lost it, and after that I was never quite sure which finger I had
used last. I couldn't lick off a letter after using it, for while
that would have made success certain, it would also have
provoked too much curiosity. There was curiosity enough without that. To the audience, I seemed more interested in my
fingernails than I was in my subject; one or two persons asked
afterwards what was the matter with my hands.

" 'It was then that the idea of pictures occurred to me!
Then my troubles passed away. In two minutes I made six
pictures with my pen, and they did the work of the eleven
catch-sentences and did it perfectly. I threw the pictures away
as soon as they were made, for I was sure I could shut my
eyes and see them any time. That was a quarter of a century
ago; the lecture vanished out of my head more than twenty
years ago, but I could rewrite it from the pictures—for they
remain.' "

Twenty-five years had passed, Mark Twain had long since
forgotten the *words* he had used, but his *mental images* still
remained so strong that he could reproduce that lecture from
the pictures! If these pictures remained so strong after a quarter of a century, do you think there was any danger of his
forgetting what he wanted to say while he was on the platform?

I myself am far from being a trained public speaker, yet I
have given hundreds of lectures to clubs, corporations, and
conventions all over the United States and Canada, and I have

never used notes. I have trained dozens and dozens of businessmen to get up on their feet at conferences and conventions and
remember what they wanted to say, without once having re-
course to written notes or visible reminders. And without ex-
ception, these men have reported that the ability to talk straight
to their associates, without having to fumble over bits of paper
or shuffle with memoranda, has doubled the attention and respect of their audiences. That is only to be expected. There is
something that is irresistibly compelling about the man who
can look you straight in the eye and say what he wants to say,
without hesitancy, and with purpose and assurance.

Some time ago, Congressman Harold Cooley of North Carolina delivered a speech before a group of industrialists, urg-
ing them to move their factories to North Carolina. Naturally,
he had to point out to these manufacturers the special induce-
ments his state has to offer as a home of industry. He spoke
forcefully and convincingly, and without notes. Here are the
points he covered:

The advantages North Carolina offers to industry are:

1. Ample economical power.
2. Moderate climate.
3. Plentiful raw materials.
4. Business-minded legislation.
5. Efficient native-born labor.
6. Excellent transportation facilities.
7. Strategic location.

I mentioned that Congressman Cooley spoke without notes. That is because he used this Mental Filing System. Here is how he "visualized" each point:

1. Ample economical power (alarm clock). Most alarm clocks are cheap articles to buy. They are economical. Winding them requires only the power of your arm muscles, of which you have an *ample* amount. There is always ample power to run an alarm clock by electricity, and it is *economical* to use.

2. Moderate climate (trousers). See a pair of your summer trousers, made of white duck or linen. These are worn only in a moderate climate. You wear them *climb*ing mountains.

3. Plentiful raw materials (chair). The chair is built of knotted, unpainted, unplaned, raw wood, and is bound in rawhide. It is piled high and plentifully with raw fruit and vegetables, and there's a piece of red raw meat resting on the raw materials. Moreover, it's a *raw*king chair.

4. Business-minded legislation (table). A committee of the big businessmen of your city are arguing business problems around the table. They are busily wrapping their legs around the legs of the table, and telling each other to *mind* their own *business*.

5. Efficient native-born labor (newspaper). See a newborn *native* baby lying on a copy of a labor paper, holding a fish. It looks like John L. Lewis, the *labor* leader.

6. Excellent transportation facilities (automobile). The automobile is an *excellent* means of *transportation*; it facilitates transportation because it can go practically anywhere. Picture an automobile smashing up first a train, then a transport plane.

7. Strategic location (policeman). A traffic policeman is always stragetically located so he can command all points. His legs are straddled over the *location*, and he directs local traffic. In enforcing the law, he must use *strategy*.

This list is probably the most difficult in the book, for the points are abstract in meaning. But let's see how many of them you can recall, after one careful reading:

1. ....   4. ....

2. ....   5. ....

3. ....   6. ....

          7. ....

CHAPTER FIFTEEN

BAITING YOUR MENTAL HOOKS FOR BETTER WRITING

"YES," YOU AGREE, "the Mental Filing System is great for delivering a speech without notes, but I have to write it down on paper first to organize it. I don't see how I can compose the whole thing mentally."

The ability to organize your theme without notes, to develop ideas in your mind, is one of the most valuable things this memory system can teach you. You will find it can be applied not only to speeches but to writing long letters and even articles.

Let me give you an example of the way I planned and delivered a talk several months ago, using mental notes. I was to address a group of salesmen, outlining the general principles that every man who sells for a living ought to know as well as the name of his firm. As I had done a bit of research in the subject of salesmanship, I made a mental review of the principles I had learned from my reading and observation. A list of ten rules for any salesman formed the skeleton of my talk.

I wrote them in order on a piece of paper and proceeded to file them in my Mental Filing System. Once they were filed I had no further need for the paper. This is the list:

TEN RULES OF SALESMANSHIP

1. Be prompt.
2. Be neat.
3. Don't talk about yourself.
4. Smile—be pleasant.
5. Tell the truth.
6. Don't ramble—get to the point.
7. Never argue.
8. Know your product thoroughly.
9. Be enthusiastic, and make your enthusiasm contagious.
10. Remember names and faces.

I shall not attempt to reproduce the mental images I formed to remember this list, for I am not presenting it as an exercise. However, you might try making up your own pictures on which to hang these rules.

For a few days I made use of every spare moment to expand my images for these rules. I remembered, for example, what had happened to a salesman who lost a valuable customer for his firm by failing to be on time for an appointment. So I added him to the picture I had formed for rule one, and subsequently introduced his story into my speech. Mulling over the importance of rule ten, *Remember names and faces*, I decided to tell my audience about John L. Horgan, the hotel manager who never forgets anyone's name and face. So I expanded my picture for rule ten by seeing Mr. Horgan and his hotel register behind the general-delivery window, shaking hands and calling everyone by name.

As I continued playing around with these ideas, I found to my surprise that I had enough material not only for this one speech but for a whole series of lectures, if necessary! I had baited the mental fishhooks, and the fish were coming to the surface faster than I could land them! In the end, my problem was not what to say, but what to eliminate for lack of time.

This may show you what I mean when I say that the filing of a mental outline is so valuable a part of the Mental Filing System. You see, when you write your ideas directly on paper, they tend to "jell," and you become convinced that you have said all there is to say on the subject. But when you set out your mental hooks, nibbles come right up out of your subconscious and you haul up ideas you never suspected were there.

A practical way of using this plan in writing an article is to write down eight or ten points about your topic, which you want to develop. File these on your key words and play with them in your leisure time for a week or so. Then write down the ideas which you have been turning over in your mind. Give the system a trial for several weeks, choosing and developing one topic at a time. You may well discover that you have ideas to put across that other people are eager to hear, and you will be training your mind to make use of that ninety per cent of its ability which William James said is dormant and undeveloped in the average man.

CHAPTER SIXTEEN

THE COST OF FORGETTING THE WRONG THINGS

LET US SAY you are a businessman, and one day you have a really brilliant idea about improving the sales end of your business. At the next conference you outline your idea, and it goes over with a bang. Everybody gets busy on it, and for a month the executives of your company hold meetings to work out the details.

You spend hours coining the exact phrases your salesmen are going to use. You call in an expert and pay him a resounding fee to work out a scientific formula, right down to the very gestures and the tone of voice with which these sure-fire phrases are going to be delivered. You call sales meetings of all your representatives and give them the results of all this planning and preparation. You compose pamphlets and letters to outlying agents who can't attend in person, and lay this new technique at their feet, confident that it is going to double their business, as well as your own. Everything starts off with a bang—and then fizzles out.

All your hours of conference, all your painful thinking, and all of your enthusiasm, together with the money you spent promoting the idea, are simply thrown away.

Why? Merely because the individual salesman who has to be relied upon to put this new plan into actual practice, fails to do so. Why does he fail? Because he is indifferent? Nonsense. No man is indifferent to a plan calculated to earn him more money. No, the real truth is that *he can't remember his new routine at the crucial moment of contact with the customer!*

I have seen dozens of authentically good ideas fall through in just this manner, not because they *couldn't* work, but because no one *worked* them. And practically every man in business has had a similar experience.

For example, I went to lunch not long ago with two executives of one of the biggest gas and oil companies in America. They were discussing the company's new "All-Round Service," which was aimed at giving each customer just a little more than his money's worth in mere lubricants. The company had gone to extreme pains and considerable expense to work out a routine of ten services that each station attendant could perform quickly and efficiently while waiting on the customer. These ten services were called the "All-Round Service" because they were so planned that the attendant could complete them all in one circling of the car.

It had seemed a splendid idea—and it was. It had been

widely advertised, and showed every promise of pleasing customers, creating good will, and, naturally, increasing sales.

But the results in actual practice were disappointing. It was
the same old story—the service men had been provided with a
chart, showing them what to do, but they had failed to learn it.
And a chart tacked to the inside wall of the station was of little
use to them while they were outside filling up the tank.

I said: "Well, what are these ten services your men can't
remember?" And just as I suspected, these two executives
looked at each other inquiringly, and then began to laugh. They
couldn't remember them either!

I've told this story here only because it is so typical of what
is happening every day in American business, even among
the biggest and most efficient corporations.

As one businessman to another, let me ask you: does it make
sense for a firm to spend time and money and effort in working
out ways and means of improving its service, unless it also
goes the whole way to see that these improvements are carried
out? And how can they possibly be carried out unless each
individual knows exactly what he is supposed to do? And how
can he know what he is supposed to do, if he can't remember?

*We remember only what we know—we know only what we
remember.*

You, of course, having mastered ten key words of this
Mental Filing System. would be able to learn all the steps of
the "All-Round Service" in no more than ten minutes. Would
you like to prove it? Here they are:

"ALL-ROUND SERVICE"

As the station attendant steps to the car to receive the driver's order, he is supposed to:

1. Polish left half of windshield.

2. Ask, "Fill up with Ethyl?"

3. Screw cap tightly on gasoline tank, to avoid spilling.

4. Clean rear window.

5. Check tires as circle of car is made.

6. Polish right half of windshield.

7. Clean headlight lenses.

8. Service the radiator.

9. Ask, "Check your oil, sir?"

10. Ask, "Does your battery need water?"

Now, you already know that these ten services are going to be performed as you circle the car. The driver sits on the left, so as you step up to him you will naturally reach out to polish the *left* windshield. Therefore, we can simplify Service 1 by remembering just *windshield*. As you form the associations, imagine yourself circling the car. It will give you extra help.

1. (alarm clock). See bunches of shining, polished *alarm clocks* hung all over the windshield. They're so bright they dazzle your eyes. Reach out and *polish left half of windshield* with alarm clock.

2. (trousers). Ethel's *trousers* (your cousin Ethel, or your Aunt Ethel—everybody knows an Ethel) have been dipped in Ethyl gasoline. Ethel is soaked, and her *trousers* pockets are filled with Ethyl gasoline. *Ask, "Fill up with Ethyl?"*

3. (chair). See a *gasoline* can teetering back and forth on a rocking *chair*. You rush over to screw down the cap to stop the gasoline from slopping over on the *chair*. *Screw cap on gasoline tank*, to avoid spilling.

4. (table). You carry a *table* around to the back of the car; then you climb up on the *table* to reach the rear window. *Clean rear window.*

5. (newspaper). *Newspapers* are plastered all over the tires, and you can't pull them off. The *newspaper* headline reads: TIRE BURSTS—FIVE KILLED. All cars should have *five* tires, including the spare. *Check tires.*

6. (automobile). The license number *666,666* has been written all over the windshield with chalk. You scrub it off

with a rag wrapped around a toy automobile (feel it), one *six* at a time. You can see the reflection of an *automobile* in the polished windshield. *Polish right half of windshield.*

7. (policeman). See the glare of the headlights flooding millions of *policemen,* who signal you to stop. A *policeman* is scrubbing the headlight lenses. *Clean headlight lenses.*

8. (revolving door). The *revolving doors* are stuffed with radiators hissing and boiling over, and steam shoots out of the *revolving door. Service the radiator.*

9. (mailbox). The *mailbox* is coated with oil, and oil is dripping out of it as you slide a check in the slot. The check gets soaked with greasy oil from the *mailbox. Ask, "Check your oil, sir?"*

10. (general-delivery window). A battery stands in the *general-delivery window,* with wires attached to the bars of the window. Sparks shoot out of the *general-delivery window,* and you douse it and the battery with water. *Ask, "Does your battery need water?"*

Now without glancing back, write the ten steps of the "All-Round Service" below. This is not a skip-about test, since the essence of the "All-Round Service" is its sequence.

1. . . . .
6. . . . .
2. . . . .
7. . . . .
3. . . . .
8. . . . .
4. . . . .
9. . . . .
5. . . . .
10. . . . .

CHAPTER SEVENTEEN

THE STUDENT REMEMBERS THROUGH SCHOOL AND COLLEGE

1 WAS SITTING on my front porch one day when a couple of the neighbor boys walked up the path. Something was on their minds, and it didn't take them long to tell me about it. Their teacher had told them to learn the thirteen original states of the Union as their history assignment for the day, and one look at that formidable list had them down. Neither of them, they admitted candidly, was a star pupil as it was, and—well, they wanted to go fishing. If they could only find a way of memorizing those states quickly. . . . They beat around the bush, like Tom Sawyer, for a while, and then one of them came to the point.

"Do *you* know the thirteen original states?" he asked.

I had to admit I didn't, and his face fell.

"Heck," he said. "Pop said you were a memory expert or something."

"Well," I said, "I don't know them now, but I'd like to learn them. Suppose you run home and get your book, and we'll memorize them together."

"Can you teach us by tomorrow?" they wanted to know.

"I'll teach you this afternoon, and you'll have time to go fishing besides."

They were back with the book in no time. I began by explaining the first thirteen key words and the way they were used to hook up images and associations. They mastered these easily, finding them vastly entertaining. Then we went on to work up associations for each state. The boys were bristling with interest as they discovered for the first time that memorizing can be fun instead of drudgery.

After they had learned the associations, I had them recite the whole list to me three or four times. Then I closed the book and said, "You fellows recite that list several times between now and class tomorrow. Most important, run over it the last thing before you go to sleep tonight. Now you'd better run along and attend to your fishing."

The next afternoon they returned, glowing. Not only had both recited the states perfectly, but one of them, flushed with self-confidence, had volunteered to reel them off *backwards*, and his performance had gone off without a hitch.

These two are now using the Mental Filing System in their school work wherever the lesson calls for the memorizing of lists or data. And while neither is at the head of his class, their teachers report a marked improvement in their work.

Here I should like to meet a question which crops up now and then when I recommend teaching this system to school-children. *Does information memorized by this method stay in the mind as long as that learned by the old method of endless repetition?* Yes, definitely yes. In fact, it is remembered even longer. When we employ special devices to retain certain bits of knowledge, they rarely escape us. Consider how the rhyme "Thirty days hath September" helps us remember instantly the number of days in any month. And if I should suddenly ask you whether it is safe to eat oysters in April, you could tell me immediately.

You may be interested to know just what associations we used in memorizing the thirteen original states. Perhaps you will want to try it yourself. Here they are.

THE THIRTEEN ORIGINAL STATES

(in the order of their admission to the Union)

1. Delaware	8. South Carolina
2. Pennsylvania	9. New Hampshire
3. New Jersey	10. Virginia
4. Georgia	11. New York
5. Connecticut	12. North Carolina
6. Massachusetts	13. Rhode Island
7. Maryland	

1. Delaware (alarm clock).   The *alarm* goes off—"Beware! *Della* beware!" See *Della wea*ring an *alarm clock* tied around her neck, screaming, "Beware! Beware!" Alarm clocks bobbing up and down in Delaware River.

2. Pennsylvania (trousers).   Trousers are pants—
*Pant*sylvania. Clotheslines filled with *trousers* crowd the
halls of the *Pennsylvania* Station, and on the *Pantsylvania*
railroad train, *trousers* blow out of every *second* window.

3. New Jersey (chair).   See your new *jersey* sweater hanging over the back of the *chair*. A *Jersey* cow sits on the *chair*
trying to pull the *jersey* sweater over her head, and her
horns tear holes in the *jersey* on the *chair*.

4. Georgia (table).   *George* Washington, King *George* of
England, and *George* Bernard Shaw are having a conference around your dining-room *table*. As each *George* tries
to get across a point he bangs his fist on the *table*. See a
beautiful *Georgia* peach eating juicy *Georgia* peaches at
the *table*.

5. Connecticut (newspaper).   See the front page of a
Connecticut newspaper. There's a picture of the *Connecticut*
Yankee at King Arthur's Court cutting the throat of his
girl friend *Conn*ie. The large letters of the *newspaper*
headline read *CONNIE'S NECK IS CUT*. You are cutting
up the Connecticut newspaper.

6. Massachusetts (automobile).   There is a *mass* of automobiles piled up. A priest is celebrating *Mass* before a con-
gregation of *automobiles*. The automobile is messy
(massy). It has Massachusetts license on it.

7. Maryland (policeman). The big *policeman* and *Mary* Pickford are singing a duet, "*Maryland*, my *Maryland*." The policeman hits her with his night stick, and *Mary lands* on the ground.

8. South Carolina (revolving door). The sun is shining through the *revolving door* making palm trees spring up inside, for the *revolving door* has gone *South*. Your Aunt Caroline sits in one of the partitions of the *revolving door*, mopping her face under the *Southern* sun.

9. New Hampshire (mailbox). You try to push a *new ham* into the *mailbox*, but the little slot *hampers* you. See the *mailbox* dripping with grease from the *new ham* that came from *New Hampshire*. The grease drips from the *mailbox* into a *new hamper* below.

10. Virginia (general-delivery window). The *Virgin* Queen, Queen Elizabeth, is singing through the *general-delivery window*. Her song is "Carry me back to old *Virginny*," and Virginia accompanies her by strumming on the bars of the *general-delivery window*.

11. New York (sidewalk). This is easy. See the crowd on the *New York sidewalks*, singing, "The *Sidewalks* of *New York*."

12. North Carolina (elevator). The *elevator* is going up *North*. The *elevator* boy is a darkie from *North Carolina*

who is singing *carols* while he takes the *elevator* up *North*. Everyone on the *elevator* is waving *North Carolina* pennants.

13. Rhode Island (floor).   See an *island* in the center of the *floor*. A *road* runs along the *floor* right through the *island*, and *thirteen Rhode Island* red hens are pecking through the *road* to get at the *floor*. A *Rhode Island* red *rooster* is crowing in the middle of the *floor*.

Longer lists, such as the forty-eight states, can be mastered in the same way by using more key words. (Key words up to 100 will be found in the appendix at the end of this section.)

Test yourself in the spaces below to see how well you know the thirteen original states:

1. . . . .   7. . . . .

2. . . . .   8. . . . .

3. . . . .   9. . . . .

4. . . . .   10. . . . .

5. . . . .   11. . . . .

6. . . . .   12. . . . .

        13. . . . .

On many occasions through his school and college career a student is required to have at his finger tips certain selected groups of facts. We all know only too well how often a question in an examination asks us to *"Name five causes of . . ."* or *"Present, in order, the events leading up to . . ."* When you realize that at least half of the average examination questions in physics, chemistry, biology, history, economics, or government are of this general type—questions asking for lists or groups of facts—you will see at once the enormous value the Mental Filing System can be to the schoolchild or college student.

This use of the System may be made as well by many of us who are long out of school. Many magazine and newspaper articles nowadays are presented in such a form that we can make the Mental Filing System help us remember indefinitely what we read. The informative articles about new developments in industry or medicine, about customs in other countries, or about new departures in warfare give us facts that we can long remember if we take the trouble to file them on our key words.

Note that I do not claim that the Mental Filing System will make you remember everything you read. There is no system on earth that can pretend to do that. But the lessons you have already learned in this book will enable you to remember much of what you read in the field of science and history and in current periodicals, for the Mental Filing System helps you remember and assemble *facts*. Next time you have a copy of *The Readers Digest,* try seeing how many of the factual articles can become part of your fund of information through the use of our system of key-word association.

CHAPTER EIGHTEEN

HOW TO REMEMBER
NUMBERS

THE MENTAL FILING SYSTEM has a special application immeasurably useful to every one of us in almost every aspect of our lives—its use in remembering numbers. Telephone numbers, addresses, important dates in history, birthdays, and anniversaries are only a few of the items you'll be able to fix in your mind now that you know the key words. The ability to remember numbers sometimes means the difference between making or losing a sale or passing or flunking a course in school. You've surely known crises when a number remembered correctly would have meant everything to you.

We've shown that it is far easier for the mind to retain a vivid image than a completely abstract number. Substituting the key words for numbers, and composing a picture with them, is the trick. Here is a telephone number: 7189. Using the key words for the numbers, we get *policeman, alarm clock, revolving door, mailbox.* These form themselves into a picture readily. Close your eyes and see a *policeman throwing an*

111

alarm clock through a revolving door and hitting a mailbox.
Visualize every bit of the scene clearly—the policeman's brass
buttons dazzlingly bright, the shattered glass as the alarm clock
crashes through the revolving door, and the broken mailbox
surrounded by spilled letters. If the image is vivid enough,
you'll never forget the number: 7189.

The device is simple. Let's see if you know what famous
date in history this picture represents: from inside the general-
delivery window you watch two automobiles in a head-on colli-
sion. Get it? The date of the Norman Conquest, 1066.

The formula for remembering an anniversary is simplest of
all, for you work with three digits at most. Let us say your
wife's birthday falls on July 23. July is the 7th month, so
we'll call the date 7-23. The picture is ready for you: a policeman (7) trying to fit a pair of trousers (2) on the legs of a
chair(3). Get the image clearly in your mind, and the little
woman will never have cause to complain again.

The key words for the numbers one through nine make it
possible for you to form a picture for any number. (Since I
haven't given you a word for zero, you might use *wheel*. It's
easy to remember because a zero is round like a wheel.) However, the next chapter will give you an additional list of key
words, up to one hundred. Numbers of more than four or five
digits may be more easily retained if you use the key words
for the higher numbers, fitting fewer objects into your image.
I'll give you an example of what I mean. My automobile license
number is 428467. If I make my mental picture out of only the
first nine key words, I have to find a place for a table, a pair
of trousers, a revolving door, another table, an automobile,

and a policeman. But by breaking the license number into groups of two digits, I need use only three objects in my picture instead of six. The key word for 42 is Elephant, 84 is Light, and 67 is Bell. I remember my license number by picturing an elephant with a light tied to his trunk and a bell to his tail: 42-84-67.

But fortunately, most of the numbers that we have to remember are short ones, rarely over four digits, and the key words you already know will in general suffice to keep them in your mind. In all frankness, I don't recommend your learning the additional key words *just* to help you remember longer numbers. You might as well jot down your license and social-security numbers in your notebook.

The first ten key words are the ones you will use the most. Knowing the next five, as you do, will often help a lot, as for example in a long shopping list. I'm including the list of key words from 16 to 100 in order to make this training complete. I don't suggest your sitting down and learning them all immediately. First, go about using the first fifteen. If in a couple of months you feel that knowing associations for higher numbers would come in handy, get at the list and study the key words. Take ten at a time, learning them just as you did the first ones, and put them to work as soon as possible in your daily affairs.

CHAPTER NINETEEN

NOW YOU HAVE
100 MENTAL HOOKS!

16. MAID

17. BANANAS

18. SHOWER BATH

19. RIDING BOOTS

20. STAIRS

21. TELEPHONE

22. LIVERY STABLE

23. HORSE

24. WOODS

25. RIVER

26. FENCE

27. PASTURE

28. COW

29. PIGS

30. TURKEYS

31. FARMER

32. HOUSE

33. LAWN MOWER

34. CLOVER

35. RAKE

36. EGGS

37. DOG

38. GUN

39. MOTORCYCLE

40. RABBIT	61. HOME
41. CIRCUS	62. SUITCASE
42. ELEPHANT	63. DEPOT
43. MONKEY	64. TICKET
44. LION	65. TRAIN
45. AFRICAN TRIBE	66. SEAT
46. GIRAFFE	67. BELL
47. TRAPEZE	68. PORTER
48. BAND	69. MAGAZINE
49. CLOWN	70. PILLOW
50. CANNON	71. SMOKING ROOM
51. GYPSY	72. FACE
52. CARDS	73. HANDS
53. MERRY-GO-ROUND	74. TOWEL
54. FERRIS WHEEL	75. DINING CAR
55. ROLLER COASTER	76. ORANGES
56. HOT DOG	77. TOAST
57. PICKLES	78. COFFEE
58. PINK LEMONADE	79. MATCH
59. MONEY	80. CIGARETTE
60. WAITER	81. HOTEL

82. KEY	91. BEACH CLUB
83. ROOM	92. BATHING SUIT
84. LIGHT	93. SANDY BEACH
85. RADIO	94. SUN
86. MIRROR	95. OCEAN
87. COMB	96. BOAT
88. BRUSH	97. ROD
89. HAIR	98. REEL
90. LINEN SUIT	99. HOOK

100. SAILFISH

CHAPTER TWENTY

INTERESTING FACTS
AND HOW TO RECALL THEM

WITH YOUR LIST of key words, you can make a part of your permanent mental baggage any collection of data you wish. Obviously, usefulness will be your first criterion even in *drilling* with lists of words. Scarcely less desirable is this type of one-two-three memory as a social asset—from an also-asked you can leap easily into the proud position of the life of any party. To know the names of the first fifteen Vice-Presidents of the United States would be a curious accomplishment of no great use. On the other hand, you are constantly coming across references in books to "the sixth President" or "the eighth President," and so on. And aren't people constantly asking you, or aren't you asking yourself, "Who came after Monroe?" and so on? So, knowing the order of succession of the Presidents of the United States is a really useful accomplishment. Here are the first fifteen:

1. George Washington
2. John Adams

119

3. Thomas Jefferson
4. James Madison
5. James Monroe
6. John Quincy Adams
7. Andrew Jackson
8. Martin Van Buren
9. William Henry Harrison
10. John Tyler
11. James K. Polk
12. Zachary Taylor
13. Millard Fillmore
14. Franklin Pierce
15. James Buchanan

Of course, it's just as important to know the second group of fifteen. Interestingly enough, this second group begins with our second most famous President, Abraham Lincoln. Rather than use the 16th to 30th key words in learning this group, it is easier to think of Lincoln as the first President, and add fifteen, to get his number in the complete succession: $1 + 15 = 16$. And so on. This second list of fifteen takes you through Calvin Coolidge, and from there on unaided memory will do the rest.

Of course, in these days of flux, with world politics as much America's interest (if not business) as WPA or CCC camps, it's well to know just where things are happening. Polish up your geography. Consult *The World Almanac* for a list of the world's largest islands or longest rivers. You'll find Java among the first, the Amazon and Volga among the second. In that way, you can get at least a quantitative mind's eye picture of land and water that make news. People make news, too—first and foremost. Do you know the names of the rulers of the five greatest countries? But, for that matter, do you know the names of these countries? You'll find the lists in the omniscient *World Almanac.*

Of course, these are but samples of the kind of knowledge you can have at your instant command. Apply your key words to any situation that requires data *remembered* for the sake of your career or for the sake of your ego. Practically any factual book you pick up contains a number of related facts you will want to pick out of your mental file just like that—one, two, three, four, five!

And, if you haven't guessed it already, the key words can open up a lot of fun to you. Use them in games, combining profit with pleasure. For instance, in a group, using *The World Almanac* as a text, each person recites a list slowly, such as the last ten winners of the Kentucky Derby or the Rose Bowl champions for the past fifteen years. Allow thirty seconds for each item. Then the players, excepting the person who propounded the list, try to duplicate the items in correct order. After each person has had his turn saying a list, papers are collected, and scores totaled.

PART TWO

HOW TO REMEMBER
NAMES AND FACES

CHAPTER ONE

HOW GOOD IS
YOUR MEMORY FOR
NAMES AND FACES?

"I know your face, but I just can't remember your name."

You will admit you've had to say it often—far too often. Every time you say it to someone, no matter how hard you try to be courteous, you are stating all too plainly, *"We've met before, I know, but you didn't make enough of an impression to make me remember you."*

And both you and he are painfully aware of it. The apology is perfectly sincere, but no one will ever really forgive you the crime of forgetting him.

From a practical point of view, consider the potential friendships, business contacts, sales, and general advancement that you lose when you antagonize people by admitting that they are unimportant to you.

For the very reason that the inability to remember names is so common, the man who has the knack of tying up names with faces has vast opportunities for getting ahead of others.

125

Later I will tell you how the success of such eminent personalities as Franklin D. Roosevelt, Charles M. Schwab, and James A. Farley was enhanced by their ability to remember names and faces.

I am going to teach you how to develop your memory for names. The system is simple, and its application will bring you real rewards in every field of your life. I want to give you four rules for remembering names and faces. Actually, they are more than just rules. They are four basic, fundamental principles that, regularly applied, will enable you to fix definitely in your memory the names of the people you meet.

If that sounds too good to be true, let me tell you of some results that I have actually obtained in my classes.

An executive of a large rubber company in Akron came to me with the complaint that he simply could not remember names, although he had been able to train his memory for other details in his business. He could rarely retain even two new names at one time. This was serious, for in the ordinary course of his work he frequently had to attend conferences where he might meet eight or ten new people all at once. They naturally remembered him; he was one of the best-known men in the industry. But his inability to remember them at a second meeting was causing him increasing embarrassment and vexation. He asked me if there wasn't some technique, some *secret* I could teach him to solve his problem.

I introduced him to these four fundamental principles. He was a little doubtful at first that these simple rules could make so much difference in his memory for names, but he was willing to give them a try.

Within a few days, he was able to meet twenty people at once and remember their names later with practically no conscious effort. To him, that was the incredible part of the whole business—the realization that what had seemed a superhuman power could have become a habit almost as automatic as shaking hands.

Last season, when I was conducting a course in memory in New York City, one of my students was Miss Roslin Kennedy, daughter of the publisher of *Yachting*. Like the rubber executive, Miss Kennedy was chiefly worried about her poor memory for names. When she came to me, she had reached the point where she no longer even attempted to remember them, for she was convinced that she simply lacked any ability at all to do it.

Yet, when I gave a demonstration meeting, a week after she enrolled in the course, Miss Kennedy was able to get up on the platform and call *eighty-five* people in the audience by name! Mind you, she had known none of them previously. They were all total strangers, who had simply given her their names as they entered the auditorium.

These cases sound fantastic, but *your* memory can accomplish as much.

Before we get into these four rules, let's ascertain just how bad your present memory for names is. I am going to let you test yourself. On the following pages you will find pictures of fifteen actual people. Each subject's real name appears beneath his or her picture. Pretend you are being introduced to these fifteen people, one at a time.

Go through the group just once, but look at each picture and name once, play fair with yourself, and go on to the next person. When you have met them all, turn to the following section. There you will see the same fifteen pictures, with no names. How many do you think you will be able to recognize?

MR. PRICE

BILL WALKER

MISS DEARDEN

MR. GERMAN

MR. SOLOMON

MR. GABLE

MR. CHRISTEN

MR. CURRAN

MRS. WITHERS

CONGRESSMAN COOLEY

MR. BYRD

MR. BELL

MR. CONE

MR. BAER

MRS. MAY

YOU HAVE JUST met fifteen new faces. On the following pages you will see them again, appearing in a different order, just as you might run across them in real life.

See whether you can write the correct name under each photograph. If you can recognize eight, your memory is good; if you get twelve, it's fine. But if you remember the names of only four or five at this second meeting, bear in mind that there are many other people in the same boat with you.

Of course, if you get all fifteen correctly, we'd still like to have you with us. If you're that good to begin with, perhaps you can become even better with a few hints to make you remember faster and longer!

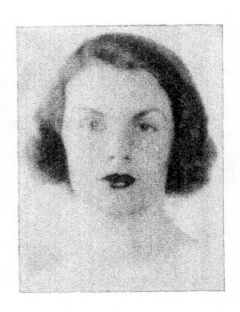

MAKE A NOTE of the number of people you just recognized among these photographs, so that you will be able to watch your improvement as you take further exercises in meeting new faces. Don't look back at these pictures, for you are going to meet some of these men and women again later on, and a backward glance now may interfere with a correct check on your future ability to remember names and faces.

CHAPTER TWO

THERE'S GOLD
IN THOSE NAMES

THE TITLE of this chapter is a general precept to observe if you are sincerely interested in remembering names. This is not one of the four separate rules for remembering names that I am going to give you. It is a preface to these, without which you could never apply them. It is the first principle you must have to become skillful in associating people with their names.

In general, we are interested in names to the extent that we are interested in their owners. If a man means anything at all to us, we usually remember his name. Here is an imaginary incident, one in which you might well figure, which will illus- trate how naturally this law of interest works.

Suppose, while you are standing in a hotel lobby with a friend, a man comes along, and your friend introduces you. You glance at the newcomer casually, pay no attention to his name, continue your conversation. The stranger has meant nothing to you; you haven't even bothered to retain his name for an instant.

However, the next time you are in that hotel lobby, your new acquaintance approaches you with the air of an old friend and asks you to lend him ten dollars.

Are you as indifferent as you were the first time you met this fellow? Hardly. You look him over carefully, studying his features with mounting interest. Finally you say, "I'm sorry, Mr. Er . . . I don't think I got your name."

"Wheeler," he says, "Bob Wheeler."

"Wheeler," you repeat slowly. "Wheeler. I suppose you spell it the usual way—W-h-e-e-l-e-r."

"That's right. Bob Wheeler."

"Well, Mr. Wheeler," you say, as you reluctantly draw ten dollars from your wallet, "I hope we meet again some time—soon."

And as months go by, and you don't hear from Mr. Bob Wheeler, you think of him often. It's no effort at all to remember his name, and as for his face, you'd recognize that if you saw it fifteen years from now in Indo-China!

His name means something to you now. It means money.

In the same way, every person you meet may mean something to you. Today's casual acquaintance may lead you to tomorrow's friend, business associate, customer, employer, husband, or wife.

So before we learn the technical rules for remembering names, we must cultivate a *desire* to remember them. We must realize that the people we meet will mean more to us if we take an interest in them. Remembering a man's name is simply a manifestation of our interest in him as a person.

If you want to make the most of your acquaintance with other people, *be name-conscious.*

The quickest way to convince a man that you fully realize his importance and value his friendship is to take the trouble to learn his name and address him by it when you speak to him. This fact was discovered more than two thousand years ago. and diplomats, businessmen, and society leaders have not improved upon it yet.

A man named Cineas demonstrated it then, when his king, Pyrrhus, sent him to Rome on a delicate mission. Pyrrhus had been making war on Rome, and now wanted peace, so he chose Cineas as the wisest and most diplomatic man at court to go to discuss terms of peace with the enemy.

Under the circumstances, Cineas was not welcomed very warmly. But he was not an ordinary man. The first thing he did upon his arrival was to ask the names of all the men in the Roman senate. Before morning he knew them all by heart.

The next day, when he rose to speak, every senator in Rome was amazed—and delighted—to discover that this stranger actually knew him by name, and mentioned him personally during his address. Naturally, Cineas was very well received.

Twenty centuries after Cineas—or, to be precise, in the presidential campaign of 1932—James A. Farley used exactly the same technique in winning voters to the cause of Franklin Delano Roosevelt and the Democratic Party. Farley, in a coast-to-coast tour, met literally thousands of citizens. He learned their names and solicited their support in person. When he returned to Washington, he sent each one a letter, greeting him by his first name. "Dear John" or "Dear Mike" was the way these letters began, and they were signed "Jim." Modern commentators on that campaign make no bones about the fact that Farley's ability to remember names (about fifty thousand is his claim) was one of the deciding factors in making that election a landslide for Roosevelt.

Roosevelt himself knows the value of being able to call people by name. When I visited the White House some time ago, Russ Wood, who is assigned to the White House detail of the Secret Service, told me how good the President's memory is in this respect. When he first came to the White House he did not meet Roosevelt for several weeks and had no idea that the chief executive could distinguish him from the dozens of other attendants on duty. Imagine his surprised pleasure when the President, on passing him one day, called out genially, "Hello there, Woodie! How are you?"

Any experienced salesman will tell you that no amount of sales talk will go so far in winning over a customer as the simple act of convincing him that you remember him and take a special interest in him. Greet a customer with, "Oh, good afternoon, Mr. Er . . . ah . . ." and you make him feel that he is just another routine prospect, one of the thousands of unimportant people you deal with day in and day out. But address him unhesitatingly by name, and you assure him immediately that you recognize him as an individual with individual needs and that he can rely on you to give him special service and consideration. Every businessman knows this well and realizes that whenever he muffs a customer's name he is jeopardizing that customer's patronage and good will.

One of my students, Louis L. Libby, a representative of Wynn Builders, Inc., gave me an illustration of the value of remembering names out of his own experience. Shortly after he took the memory course he happened to be conducting some prospective clients through one of the company's model homes at Malvern Park, Malvern, Long Island. There were three in the party, a Mr. and Mrs. Albert Lester and Mrs. Lester's mother, Mrs. Jacoby. They looked the house over, expressed interest, and said they would return later.

Mr. and Mrs. Lester did come again after several weeks, and Mr. Libby recognized them as they entered the model living room. He greeted them by name. "I'm glad to see you back again," he said. "Where's Mrs. Jacoby?" Mr. Lester looked at him with surprise, and then with admiration. "By George!" he exclaimed. "You must have talked with dozens of people since we were last here, and still you remembered our name. I'd give anything for a memory like that."

While showing them through the house again, Mr. Libby explained he had no natural gift for remembering names.

Well, the next time the Lesters visited the development they asked to see Mr. Libby, and purchased their home through him. When he told me the story, Mr. Libby said he had no doubt that he owed his commission on this sale to the fact that he won over the prospective customers by remembering their names.

The value people place on their own names is something for wonder. Consider the example of James B. Duke, who, in order to perpetuate his name, offered to endow Trinity College in Durham, North Carolina, with something over fifty million dollars if its name were changed to Duke University. This sounds like an extreme case of pride in one's name, but you will find something similar in every man. Think how flattered you would be to have a friend name his child after you. And how much extra value do you put on a gift with your name engraved or embroidered on it. Any man or woman is thrilled at the idea of having his or her name assured of permanency. Accordingly. every time you surprise someone by remembering his name, you evoke a similar pleasant emotion.

An executive's success is enhanced not only by knowing his customer's names but also by remembering those of his employees. Many have profited by the example of Charles M. Schwab, who was paid a million dollars a year for his amazing skill in handling people. He once had eight thousand employees at the Homestead Mill and was justifiably proud of knowing each one of these by name. When he revisited the mills after many years, some of the senior foremen placed bets on how many of the old-timers Schwab could remember. There were eight hundred remaining out of the eight thousand who originally worked under him, and as they filed past him to shake his hand, he called five hundred by name. He told me himself later that he could have done better if he had known he was being checked.

CHAPTER THREE

HOW TO GET
THE NAME STRAIGHT

THE CHIEF REASON you "forget" a name is that you never knew it in the first place.

Stop for a moment to think about the usual introduction. A friend of yours says, "I'd like you to meet Mr. New——m." You offer your hand and say "How do you do. Glad to meet you."

Now what is the man's name? Newsom? Newton? Newman? Newlin?

Let's repeat the introduction. The man you have just met is Mr. Newsom. His picture is on the next page. Whenever you fail to hear a name distinctly, don't let it ride, hoping you'll catch the name during the conversation. Speak up at once. Say, "I'm sorry, but I didn't get the name." Your new acquaintance won't be offended. On the contrary, you will be paying him a genuine compliment by showing him that you really want to know who he is.

If the name is unusual, or has several forms, ask how it is spelled. "Newsom without an E?" If you know someone else by

159

the same name, find out if he is related. By that time, Mr. Newsom will be getting interested in you, and he will probably break down and confess he didn't get your name either.

So, first of all, *get the name right.*

Concentrate entirely upon a person's name while you are being introduced, excluding any other impression for those few moments. Wait until you have understood his name clearly before you give any attention to his personality, voice, or clothes. Don't stop to think about what you are going to say next; don't let your mind wander for a split second. Concentrate on getting the name right.

Do you often catch your own name being mispronounced in an introduction? Are you presented as *Richards* instead of

Richardson, or *Davis* instead of *Davies?* It's an experience
you have surely noticed. Let me give you a tip. When you hear
your own name mispronounced, you are guilty of the first step
to forgetting the name of your new acquaintance. Why? Because you are listening for your own name instead of keeping
your ears open to receive the new one. A minor mispronuncia-
tion of your name is just one of many things that may distract
you during an introduction. Don't let it happen again. Shut out
all irrelevant stimuli, and *get the name right.*

CHAPTER FOUR

THE KIND OF
REPETITION THAT
RAPS IT IN

AFTER YOU have observed Rule One: *Get the Name Right*, you must apply Rule Two: *Rap the Name in by Repetition*.

While you are talking to your new acquaintance, use his name as frequently as you can. Tack it on the end of sentences; begin your remarks to him by addressing him directly by name. Each time you speak his name aloud, you are driving it by one more hammer blow deeper into your memory. If it happens that other people are carrying on the conversation, and you cannot repeat the name aloud, then at least try saying it over and over again to yourself while you are studying your new acquaintance's features and general appearance.

And finally, when you take leave of him, use his name once more as you say good-by. Don't just say, "Glad to have met you," and let it go at that. Give him a royal send-off. Say, "Glad to have met you, *Mr. Newsom*. I hope we shall meet again." Take a final look at Mr. Newsom, at the same time making a heroic resolution that the next time you see that face, you will know that it belongs to Mr. Newsom—spelled N-E-W-S-O-M—and to no other person in the world. Stop. Did you look at Mr. Newsom? If not, do it now.

I can't impress upon you too strongly the importance of this principle of repetition. In the beginning, you will have to make a conscious effort to apply it, but as times goes on, you will find yourself doing it automatically. If you don't bother to repeat a name over and over—if you "trust to your memory" after hearing a name only once—you are not playing fair with yourself. You are not giving your memory a break; you are not "exercising" the new impression you want your mind to seize upon and retain for your future reference.

Many people who know from experience that they must give their memories every possible kind of assistance actually go so far as to write a new name down as soon as they get an opportunity. Napoleon III used this method with outstanding success. He attained the throne only after a political struggle, and realized that one way of enhancing his popularity and strengthening his position was to pay his subjects the subtle compliment of never forgetting their names. Therefore, as soon as he found himself alone after an audience, he wrote the name on a slip of paper, studied it a moment with undivided attention, and threw away the paper.

This technique is undoubtedly successful, but it is not practical enough for our general use. I think most of us would do better to rely on the homespun method of repeating the name aloud as often as we can while we are with its owner, and trying to visualize it in our minds as we do so. By all means write it down later, if you have a chance to do so. Maybe you would like to keep a record of all the new people you meet.

Even after we have repeated the name a number of times and perhaps written it out, we can give our memories one more jolt. We can review the name at any point later in the day when we collect our reminiscences of the day's events. It is a valuable technique endorsed by Theodore Roosevelt himself. Think of that man who came to your office early this afternoon. Remember his appearance and manner; and, most important, repeat his name to yourself.

A salesman can make good use of this rule of repetition and review to fix in his mind the many people he meets in a sales call. One of the best salesmen I know, a man in the hosiery business, applies it in every store he visits. He goes out of his way to remember not only the names of the buyer and assistant buyer, but the names and faces of the salespeople as well. He does it by saying the names over to himself after he leaves the store—Mr. Johnson, Miss Carter, Mrs. Franklin, Miss Bryce. It's an effort, but he knows it's worth it.

His competitor, on the other hand, doesn't trouble himself to remember anyone but the buyer, the person who signs the orders. Accordingly, when a customer asks which line of hosiery is the better, whose line do you think the salesgirl pushes—the line of the salesman who rushes past her to interview the buyer, or that of the man who stops by her counter to say, "Hello there, Miss Carter? How are things going today?"

The extra minutes you spend reviewing the names of people you meet are the minutes that will mean money to you eventually.

Since repetition is so vitally important, let's turn back once more to the photograph of Mr. Newsom. You will be asked to recognize him when you encounter him in the picture tests later on, so pause for a moment to do these three things:

1. Study the photograph carefully.
2. Repeat the name aloud five times.
3. Write the name on a piece of paper.

Remember, if you want to keep a name in your mind, there is no rule more important than Rule Two: *Rap the Name in by Repetition.*

CHAPTER FIVE

FASTENING FACES
IN YOUR MIND

YOU ARE STILL in the company of your new acquaintance.
Having applied Rule One successfully, you are sure of his
name, and you are conscientiously observing Rule Two, which
means you are seizing every opportunity of saying his name
aloud. Rule Three comes next, and you are to put it into effect
at once. *Fasten the Face in Your Mind.*

The difference between the man with an excellent memory
for faces and the man who constantly mistakes one person for
another is not a matter of eyesight or of intelligence. It is a
difference in *observation.* The first man thinks about what he
is seeing; the other does not. William P. Sheridan, one of the
most celebrated detectives that ever operated in America, developed the "camera eye" to such an extent that he could pick
out of a crowd any one of twenty-two thousand criminals whose
pictures were on file with the New York police. His secret?   .
He had schooled his mind to register every detail that his eye
took in. He had learned to pay attention, to observe.

You can't get a definite picture of a man if you are thinking of anything else. You will never be able to remember faces as long as you are flustered at introductions, getting only a blurred impression of the face before you. It is absolutely necessary to forget yourself just for a few seconds to give all your attention to stamping a new portrait on your mind. It's easy for me to say, "Don't be self-conscious," I know, and I also know that a voluntary attempt to forget oneself is one of the hardest things in the world to do. But here is a suggestion to you who so often miss new impressions out of sheer self-consciousness. You might look at it as an exercise in this third rule: *Fasten the Face in Your Mind.*

Go to the movies. It's dark there, and you can forget about yourself thoroughly as you scrutinize the faces on the screen. Analyze the appearances of the actors and actresses, giving particular attention to hair, eyes, ears, noses, mouths. Try to figure out the ages of the different characters, notice their height and their gait. When a close-up flashes on the screen, watch out for wrinkles, moles, and warts. Keep your ears wide open for the quality of the voices. For name practice, you might see if you can remember later what the actors were called in the play. Most of us know we saw Myrna Loy or Clark Gable in a particular picture, but we rarely remember the names of the characters they portrayed.

The beauty of this practice is that no one has to know what you are doing, and you alone may be the judge of your results. Students who have tried it have found that it has improved their powers of observation to the degree that they carried over the quickened interest into everyday life and were able to observe without any embarrassment the faces of people to whom they were introduced.

You might practice fastening faces in your mind while you are riding in a bus or subway. Glance at the person opposite you, look in a different direction, and try to reconstruct his face in your mind. As you grow more expert you will need less and less time to take in details of physiognomy.

On the next page is a photograph of Mr. Byrd, whom you met in our first exercise. He is a member of the distinguished Virginia family that produced Admiral Richard Byrd and Senator Harry Byrd. Let's try to fasten his face in our minds.

What is your first impression of Mr. Byrd? Well, he's not a young man, nor is he extremely old. Let's call him middle-aged. His hair is gray. It's thick and wavy and curls up on top of his head like the crest of a bird. (That's an intentional pun.)

He is clean-shaven. His eyebrows are thick and bushy, and he has a mole over his left eye. These are probably the first things you will notice about Mr. Byrd. But now let's go on.

Analyzing his features more minutely, we see that his eyes are keen, penetrating, and very much alive. From the photograph, we should judge they are either gray or blue in color.

His nose is short and broad—you might call it pugnacious. His mouth is wide and thin, and turns upwards at the left corner. His chin is short, but it juts out in a strong, assertive manner.

Now notice the lines on Mr. Byrd's face. There are deep furrows in the cheeks, and there are strong lines between the eyes and on the forehead.

Mr. Byrd has a face of strong character. Look at that face until you feel absolutely confident that you could enter a room crowded with people, and pick out Mr. Byrd at a glance. Then draw upon your imagination and see if you could recognize Mr. Byrd if he were dressed differently. Imagine him wearing

glasses. Picture him with a hat and coat on. Try to visualize him as he might look dressed in overalls.

Now put the book aside and close your eyes. Try to "see" Mr. Byrd's face, against your closed lids. If the image refuses to come, pick up the book again and repeat the exercise until you see Mr. Byrd just as clearly as you see his picture in the book.

You will become rapidly more proficient in taking in a person's entire appearance in a few glances as you continue to fasten faces in your mind. Your eye can take in a hundred details at once. It is your brain which needs training in realizing what the eye has seen. Once you get the habit of concentrated observation you will take new notice of the differences between people. When you meet a man you will not be content with noting just that he is a fat man or a thin man, an old man or a young man. You will make a note of the color and quantity of his hair. You will jot down in your mental notebook whether his complexion is ruddy, swarthy, pallid, or tanned. You will pay sharp attention to peculiarities of his features, walk, manner, and voice. And so doing, you will effectively put into use Rule Three: *Fasten the Face in Your Mind.*

CHAPTER SIX

WHAT'S IN A NAME— TO REMEMBER IT BY?

Anchoring the Name by Association

OUR FOURTH, and last, basic principle for remembering names and faces is *association*. We must anchor a new name to our minds by as many other related facts, pictures, or impressions as we can hitch to it.

Let us imagine, for example, that I lead you into a room full of people and introduce you to four men in succession— Mr. Graham, Mr. Singleton, Mr. Tucker, and Mr. Wetherby. If you are making no effort to catch these names as I introduce you, three of these men will remain complete blanks to you. The fourth name, however—Wetherby—will crash in your consciousness like a cymbal. Why? Simply because your mother's maiden name happened to be Wetherby, your own middle name is Wetherby, and somewhere in the country, to your certain knowledge, you have a large assortment of uncles, aunts, cousins, nieces, and nephews, all named Wetherby.

173

Maybe this Wetherby is one of your clan. You can't help notic-
ing that name, and you have no difficulty whatever in remembering it, because it has been firmly established in your mind
since earliest childhood, and is anchored there by hundreds of
associations.

Let's suppose, on the other hand, that your mother's name
wasn't Wetherby, and that you've never known a single
Wetherby in your life. Then the name means nothing more to
you than any other three-syllable name, and you will have
to apply every rule in the game to remember it. You will have to
build up an artificial association. But how can you do it?

The easiest and best way would be to form a mental picture.
What does the sound of the name suggest to you? WEATHER-
BEE. Instantly you see Mr. Wetherby out in stormy *weather*,
trying to beat off the attack of an angry *bee*. You see this picture as you study his face, as you repeat his name, as you apply
the other rules we have been discussing. Even as you are shaking hands and saying, "How do you do, Mr. Wetherby," your
mind may already be flashing the mental picture with which
it will always associate the name *Wetherby*.

Don't get the erroneous idea that applying these rules is
going to take so much time and thought that you won't have
any left over to devote to conversation. Once you have mastered the rules thoroughly, you will find that the application
of them becomes second nature. After all, it doesn't take time
to analyze a man's face, for you have to look at him while you
are talking to him, anyway. And it doesn't take time to repeat
his name, for it is only courtesy to address him when you
speak to him. And you will find that picture associations, in

just the same way, will occur to you naturally, without inter
ruption of your other thoughts.

Let us go back, however, to our imaginary gathering. You
now know Mr. Wetherby, but you become suddenly conscious
of the fact that, although you met three other men, you don't
know one of their names. I repeat them to you again—Mr.
Graham, Mr. Singleton, and Mr. Tucker. Understanding a
little more now about the principle of association, you turn
your imagination loose. In less than one minute by the clock
you have all three names down pat—all done by association.
Something like this:

Mr. Graham: Graham crackers. *Graham* bread. *Gray ham.*
With the speed of a lightning flash, your mind shows you a
picture of *Mr. Graham* munching on *Graham crackers* while
he slices off a piece of *gray ham* to put between the *Graham*
bread. You have hooked *Mr. Graham's* name up with the
name of a nationally known product *which was already
established in your mind.*

Mr. Singleton: Mr. Singleton is *single,* he's a bachelor. He's a
singular man. He *sings* only one note, a *single tone.* See
Mr. Singleton all alone, *single, singing* one note, a *single
tone. Mr. Singleton.*

Mr. Tucker: Little Tommy Tucker sings for his supper. *Mr.
Tucker* is a fat man. He has to *tuck* in his waistline. See him
tucking in his waistline while he sings for his supper.

It goes without saying that you must be careful to tie up each one of these associations with the right person, or naturally you will begin to confuse one with the other. Name alone is not enough. Face, name, and mental picture must all be parts of one whole impression.

You will doubtless recall that when we were discussing association in connection with the Mental Filing System, we emphasized the fact that a lot of these mental pictures seem pretty ridiculous in the cold light of day. Some people are squeamish about remembering new friends by such absurd and farfetched associations, because they feel there is something basically rude about it. But let me remind you that forgetting a man's name is ruder still, and that naturally you are not going up to Mr. Graham and explain candidly that you remember his name by picturing him eating Graham crackers! While it is tactful to remember a man's name by any means at your disposal, it is more tactful still to keep those means to yourself.

When several associations occur to you, as they frequently will, don't throw away one because another one seems better. So far as association is concerned, it's a case of the more the merrier. Two hooks, or associations, are better than one, and three are better than two. You will realize this at once if you think of these associations as floating buoys by which to locate the thing you want to remember, and with which you want to pull it up to the surface of your mind.

When we meet a man for the first time, therefore, we would do well to keep our eyes and ears open for the following possibilities in the line of association:

1. Do we know somebody else by the same name?

This need not be a personal friend. We are familiar with hundreds of names of celebrities, politicians, movie stars, big businessmen, historical characters, fictional characters, and even nationally advertised products, which easily lend themselves to rapid and vivid associations. How, for example, would you associate the name of a man who happened to be called: *Heinz, Jolson, Morgan, Gable, Woollcott, Ripley, Chrysler, Booth, Peary, Ford, Coolidge, Hamilton, Lee, Vanderbilt, Dickens, Landon, Firestone, Chaplin, Jefferson, Thackeray, Winchell, Stimson, Van Doren?*

2. Do we know anything about the man himself?

If we know nothing about him in advance, frequently a few minutes' conversation will bring out many background facts which will prove helpful—his business, birthplace, home address, hobbies, etc. *Mr. Stone* may be a *contractor; Mr. Evans* may have been born in *Evansville, Indiana; Mr. Woods* may live on *Grove Street; Mr. Parr* may play *golf.* These illustrations may seem hand-picked, but you will actually encounter such combinations rather frequently *if you are on the lookout for them.*

3. Does he resemble anyone else?

Again, this doesn't have to be a personal friend of yours. A man without a chin may remind you at once of Andy Gump. The salesman with the big nose may look, if not act, like Jimmy Durante. The little man with the domineering wife may bring to mind Mr. Milquetoast. The ambitious boy just out of college may wear horn-rimmed glasses that immediately suggest Harold Lloyd. These physical characteristics will help you to remember the face by association. but you must be careful to fasten the name securely with other strings.

4. Can you connect the name with a slogan, an allusion, or a familiar quotation?

This is easier to do, of course, if you have a natural flair for puns. Here are a few illustrations I chose at random from among the membership of the Sales Executives Club of New York City:

Kaufman—Not a *cough* in a carload.

Camp—Tenting tonight on the old *camp* ground.

Hastings—*Haste* makes waste. The battle of *Hastings*.

Lane—Swingin' down the *lane*. It's a long *lane* that has no turning.

Cobb—Corn on the *cob*. (Also *Ty Cobb, Irvin Cobb*.)

Kelly—Anybody here seen *Kelly*?

Burg—Ice *burg* SOS.

Ballew—"The wind she *ballew* lak hurricane."

Sands—Footsteps in the *sands* of time.

Hull—The *hull* truth and nothing but the *hull* truth.

Arthur—King *Arthur* and his Round Table.

Boyle—A watched kettle never *boils*.

Shaw—*Shaw* me the way to go home. (Also *G. B. Shaw*.)

Lowen—"The *lowen* herd winds slowly o'er the lea."

Stech—A *stech* in time saves nine.

Surface—Save the *surface* and you save all.

5. Does the name lend itself readily to impromptu rhymes of your own making?

Making up nonsensical rhymes is not only a lot of fun, but you are apt to take such pride in the authorship that forgetting them becomes a psychological impossibility.

For example:

Mr. Barton smokes a *carton*.

Mr. Dewey's full of *hooey*.

Mrs. Shelton's got a *belt on*.

Mr. Hallett wields a *mallet*.

Mr. Hughes chews.

Mr. Hawes makes the *laws*.

Mr. Rand beats the *band*.

Mr. McLean is always *clean*.

Mr. Siegel sees an *eagle*.

Miss Raleigh is oh so *jolly*.

6. Can you make a mental picture of the name?

This, of course, is what we did with Mr. Wetherby, Mr. Graham, Mr. Singleton, and Mr. Tucker. Long names which seem to mean nothing in their entirety can frequently be broken up into syllables which do mean something. For example, the students in one of my classes found it practically impossible to remember the name *Bowkowski*. I told them to break the name up into syllables—BOW-KOW-SKI, and imagine Mr. Bowkowski *bow*ing to a *cow* with *ski*s on. This is about as mad as mental association can get, but no one had trouble with the name after that. Another of my classes had difficulty in remembering a student with a French name—*Antoine*. When this name is pronounced quickly, it sounds something like *Ant-wine*. So we imagined Mr. *Antoine* picking *ants* out of his *wine!* The picture—and the name—clicked.

These are only six out of an infinite number of ways of anchoring a name by association. More will occur to you as you put this fourth rule into use. Unlike the first three, this last rule is one you can work on even after you have left the presence of the new face. The more you do it, the more sure you may be of retaining the name. So don't overlook the value of Rule Four: *Anchor the Name by Association.*

This fourth rule has a special use which I'd like to pass on to you. You may invoke it to make others remember *your name.* If you can find an unusual way to make a potential client or customer remember your name before any other in your field, you will improve your chance of succeeding with him. Giving a prospect your card may be a good idea, but every one else does that too, and the recipient usually throws it away. If you can anchor your name in his mind through association, you'll be more likely to hear from him again.

TO REPEAT

RULE ONE (Attention) : GET THE NAME RIGHT.

RULE TWO (Repetition) : RAP THE NAME IN BY REPETITION.

RULE THREE (Observation) : FASTEN THE FACE IN YOUR MIND.

RULE FOUR (Association) : ANCHOR THE NAME BY ASSOCIATION.

CHAPTER SEVEN

MEET THREE LADIES
AND TWELVE GENTLEMEN

YOU NOW KNOW as much about the basic principles of remembering names and faces as any person alive today. You have it all at your finger tips—all that remains is practice.

You've learned the four rules and know the general principle of being name-conscious. Now to practice applying them. In much the same way as we went over Mr. Byrd's photograph a couple of chapters ago, we shall now meet the pictures of fifteen people and see how many more we can remember by applying the rules we have just learned. Every one of the four rules will not be called into use in each case, for often one or two are sufficient to make the name tie up with the face.

Most of the associations will seem grotesque, farfetched, or downright silly, but by this time you realize that it is the extraordinary, striking association that remains longest in the mind and is easiest to recall. And as you read my suggestions for remembering, try to think of some angles of your own, for in a coming chapter you will be on your own and will have to practice the principles I have taught you without props.

Mr. Price

This is Mr. Price, a very distinguished gentleman. He has paid the *price* of hard work to become president of his company. Mr. Price seems to be well to do; he has the *price*.

Notice his regular features, his keen. kindly eyes, his luxuriant white hair and mustache. Perhaps Rule Two will help most in remembering Mr. Price: repeat his name several times while you study his face.

Bill Walker

Here's Bill Walker. Doesn't he look like a regular guy who might live on your block? He is a very fast Walker but not related to Johnnie Walker. His name, Bill Walker, just suits him. Look at his keen eyes and bright smile. He certainly looks wide-awake. Wide-awake Walker. Nice to have met you, Bill Walker.

Miss Dearden

Ladies and gentlemen, may I present Miss Dearden. She's really a *dear*, so you ought to know her. By the way, *den* on the end of name means a *den* in the woods. So imagine Miss Dearden coming out of a *deer's den*. Concentrate on this picture until you know you will recognize Miss Dearden. Look at her and say, "Hello there, Miss Dearden." Are you the dear that was in the deer den, Miss Dearden?

Mr. German

Here's Mr. German. From his name, you're probably right in supposing that his forebears came from Germany. Can you see anything peculiarly Germanic in his appearance? Notice his light complexion, blue eyes, and round head, all features considered characteristic of German people. Mr. German's clean-shaven face and the neat appearance of his collar and tie indicate that he is a tidy kind of man. It would be hard to find any *germs* on Mr. *German*.

Mr. Solomon

This is Mr. Solomon. He's a very wise person, like King Solomon. He looks solemn. He's a solemn man. Look at him carefully. His face is round, like Old Sol. Perhaps Mr. Solomon isn't as solemn as he seems at first glance.

Mr. Gable

Wouldn't you like to meet Mr Gable? He's one of the most *able* young men I know. I think of him as Able Gable. Notice his twinkling eyes and white teeth. Pay particular attention to the formation of his eyebrows.

Yes, his name is the same as that of Clark Gable, but this Mr. Gable isn't a movie star, though his personality might register attractively on the screen. Good-by, Mr. Gable.

Mr. Christen

This is Mr. Christen. He was *christened ten* times on *Christ*mas. So Mr. Christen is a good Christian.

Mr. Curran

Now I want you to meet *Mr. Curran,* a great lover of horses. Mr. Curran curries his horse with a *curry* comb. He had a dog, but the *cur ran* away.

Mr. Curran keeps up with all *current* events. Take a look at his widely spaced eyes and his slightly uptilted nose. You might meet Mr. Curran again, and these features may distinguish him for you.

Mrs. Withers

May I introduce you to a very lovely lady, Mrs. Withers? If you talked to Mrs. Withers, you would immediately like her so well that you would become *keenly interested in remembering her name.* You would notice the final *s* on her name, so that you would *get the name right.*

Mrs. Withers will never *wither.* Mrs. Withers will be always *with us.* Study the photograph. Get a detailed mental picture of Mrs. Withers' hair, eyes, mouth, chin. Note her friendly expression.

Mrs. Withers, we hope you will be back *with us* later on. Your name will not *wither* out of our memories. Good-by, Mrs. Withers.

Congressman Cooley

Fellow constituents, may I present Congressman Cooley of North Carolina. On the hottest day in Washington, Congressman Cooley is always *cool.* His shiny hair looks as if he'd wet it to keep *cool.* Keep cool with Cooley. Not Coolidge—Cooley, like a Chinese laborer, only spelled COOLEY. Before you say good-by to Congressman Cooley (N.C.). *fasten his face in your mind.*

Mr. Byrd

Here's our friend Mr. Byrd again. You remember the way we fastened his face in our minds a short while ago. Note again the way his hair curls on top of his head like a *bird*'s crest, his bushy eyebrows, wide thin mouth, mole on his forehead, and deep furrows. Mr. Byrd has a strong face, and he has the sharp gaze of a *bird*.

Mr. Bell

How do you do, Mr. Bell. Mr. Bell is a handsome fellow: when you look at him you get a pleasant view or, as the French say, a *belle* vue. (This does seem a far-fetched way of tying up Mr. Bell's name with his face, but see if the very remoteness of the association doesn't help you remember his name.) If Mr. Bell's voice is as clear as his gaze, it should be clear as a *bell*. When you examine his features, say this jingle: *"Mr. Bell looks very well."*

Mr. Cone

This is Mr. Cone—a plain, straightforward name for this businesslike gentleman. As you scrutinize Mr. Cone's face, with the direct, serious expression, unusually black eyes, and the almost austere cast of features, repeat his name a few times. Mr. Cone. Mr. Cone. Mr. Cone. Get his name right—it's not Cohen, but *Cone*.

Mr. Baer

I'd like to have you meet Mr. Baer now. Can you think of anything about this pleasant face to remind you of a *bear?* How about Mr. Baer's grizzly hair, eyebrows, and mustache? They seem to be brown in color, like the color of a bruin *bear*. Do you think Mr. Baer's face, without the mustache and heavy brows, would look *bare?* Glad to have met you, Mr. Baer. We hope you don't mind our trying to find a resemblance between you and a grizzly *bear*.

Mrs. May

Mrs. May is as pretty as the month of *May*. You *may* see Mrs. *May* as the *May* queen some day.

Now that you have applied our four rules for remembering names and faces to these fifteen people, you'll want to see how much they helped you. You are going to meet these folks again, but you won't see their names. How much more easily do you think you will recognize them this time? Compare your score with the result you wrote down before you learned the four rules.

CHAPTER EIGHT

A LESSON IN
MISTAKEN IDENTITY

ONE DAY, in 1896, a woman visited Scotland Yard to lodge a complaint. About a week before, she said, she had answered an advertisement in a newspaper for a housekeeper for an English nobleman. Within a day or two a man appeared at her house and introduced himself as Lord Willoughby de Winton. He interviewed her, described his great country estate in magnificent terms, and intimated that if the lady accepted the position offered, she might in time be elevated above the status of a mere housekeeper.

His lordship must have been a man of persuasion, for before he left he suddenly discovered that he had "forgotten" to bring his wallet, and asked his new housekeeper to lend him a few pounds. The good lady, completely befuddled by her unexpected luck, impetuously handed over to him all the money she had in the house. His lordship accepted with profuse thanks, and wrote her a check to cover the amount.

What brought her to Scotland Yard was the baffling fact that when she presented the check at the bank, no one there had ever heard of Lord Willoughby de Winton. Gone was her rapturous vision of the future; gone was his lordship; and worse still, gone were her painfully earned savings. What did Scotland Yard make of it all?

A petty swindle of this caliber would probably not have disturbed Scotland Yard very much if it had stopped there. But within the next few days, sixteen other women turned up with the same story. Apparently Lord de Winton was operating in London on an extensive scale. A search was inaugurated, but no clue developed until one day a bobby in Victoria Street was attracted by a woman's cries. "There he is," she screamed. "That's him—Lord Willoughby de Winton!"

The man was arrested at once and brought to Scotland Yard. There he was confronted by the seventeen women who had lodged complaints. All but one of them identified him at once, with absolute certainty. He, on the other hand, registered the utmost bewilderment. What was all this about—Lord de Winton? *His* name was Beck, Adolph Beck, and he had never set eyes on any of these women before in his life.

Nevertheless, on the strength of the fact that sixteen women had identified him at sight, the law took its course, and Adolph Beck was sentenced to fourteen years in prison. He served seven years, and then was released.

But that is only the first half of the story. Two years after Adolph Beck left prison, another woman visited Scotland Yard and reported herself a victim of the same sort of swindle. The technique was identical: the advertisement, the visit, the forgotten wallet, the worthless check. Scotland Yard sent out an alarm, and soon Adolph Beck was once more in the toils of the law. Once more he protested his innocence.

The prison doors were about to clang on him a second time when something happened which caused Scotland Yard to pause and consider. A dozen more women entered complaints, but these women had been swindled *while Adolph Beck was behind bars being held for trial.* Were there two such swindlers —or was it just possible that Beck was telling the truth, after all?

Finally one woman who was a little less susceptible to charm than the others became suspicious, followed "Lord de Winton" from her home, trailed him to a pawnshop, watched him pawn her jewels, and then notified the police. The man they caught red-handed was a habitual criminal named Thomas. He, and not Adolph Beck, was Lord Willoughby de Winton.

The signatures on the checks were compared with Thomas' handwriting and proved him guilty beyond a doubt. The women concerned in both cases were called in, and they identified Thomas at once, just as promptly and as confidently as they had once pointed accusing fingers at Adolph Beck.

Poor Beck was finally released, and Parliament granted him five thousand pounds as consolation for his unjust imprisonment.

During his two ordeals, more than two dozen witnesses had identified Beck positively and without hesitation. Yet did he actually look like Thomas? As far as type went, he did. The two were about the same size; each had gray hair and wore a

mustache. Yet when they stood side by side, it was almost im·
possible to see how anyone could have mistaken one for the
other.

It would be ridiculous to say that the witnesses who wrongly
identified Beck as Lord Willoughby de Winton must have had
unusually poor memories for faces. There were too many of
them to excuse on those grounds. The story clearly illustrates
the fact that the *average* memory for faces is highly unreliable.
Ask any detective what he thinks of the general citizen's
memory. He will tell you that he would rather rely on one
complete set of accurate physical measurements to identify
a criminal than on the unanimous and concerted recognition
given by an entire neighborhood.

You might enjoy filling out the form the New York police
use in their efforts to trace a person who is missing or wanted
for some offense. If you were held up in New York and told
the police you could identify the robber, they would ask you
to fill out this "pedigree" form. To test your own powers of·
observation, pretend you are trying to help the police locate
some person you met very recently. It might be the telephone
repairman who came in this morning, the salesman who waited
on you in a department store, or the friend of your luncheon
companion who stopped for a brief chat at your table. How
many of the following questions could you answer?

POLICE DEPARTMENT
CITY OF NEW YORK

PEDIGREE

Color............................ Complexion ....

Age.............. Sex................ Height................ Weight................

CHECK RELEVANT MATTER

APPEARS—Slim   Stout   Medium   Drug User
    Face Pockmarked

SHOULDERS—Straight   Round   Hunchback   Stooped
    Is Right   or Left   Handed

EYES—Blue   Grey   Hazel   Brown   Maroon
    Wears Glasses   Cross-eyed: Right   or Left   Eye
    Artificial: Right   or Left   Eye
    Blind: Right   or Left   Eye

HAIR—Sandy   Blonde   Brown   Red   Auburn
    Black   Partially Grey   Grey   Partially Bald
    Bald   Wig

NOSE—Small   Large   Pug   Straight   Hooked

EARS—Small   Large   Medium   Flaring   Close to Head
    Cauliflower: Right   or Left   Both
    Deaf: Right   or Left   Both

MUSTACHE—Color .... Long   Short
    Stubby   Turned-up Ends   Pointed Ends

SPEECH—Fast Talker   Slow Talker   Stammers   Accent
    Kind.......................... Soft Voice   Gruff Voice
    Effeminate Voice   Tongue-tied

DISTINCTIVE MARKS—Note below All Scars, Tattoo Marks, Missing Teeth, Gold Teeth, Upper or Lower Jaw; If Lame, the Cause; Amputations, Bow-Legged, Knock-Kneed, Pigeon-Toed, Twitching of Features:

....

....

....

Now try filling out the form for:

1. A friend you see constantly.
2. Someone—a former classmate perhaps—whom you used to know well but have not seen in several years.
3. A person in your neighborhood whom you know only slightly.

Obviously, it is highly imperative for policemen and detectives to get a thorough training in remembering faces. In your own case it is probably not often a matter of life and death, but nevertheless whether or not you are able to remember someone's appearance may be extremely important to you, if not to the public at large. That is why a mind trained to link the right names to faces will get you a good distance ahead of the next man, for the chances are that his memory for faces is no better than the average—which we have demonstrated is distressingly poor.

Since you have had your first lesson in remembering names and faces. I suggest you try the principles out tomorrow on a few people and see how much easier people are to remember than photographs.

CHAPTER NINE

TEN NEW FACES
ALL AT ONCE

IN THIS CHAPTER you will meet ten new people. The first six will be presented with hints on how to remember them when you see them again, but after you are introduced to Mr. Rippey, Number Six, we shall leave you. There will be no clues suggested for the last four photographs, for by the time you reach them you will be able to figure out your own.

Some of these people will be presented by their full names, to give you practice in remembering first names as well as last names. The principles are just the same: you simply need a little more concentration. Try to get the first name as part of the whole picture, for knowing a man's first name or initials will often help you recall his last name—and vice versa.

Here, as in all the photographs in the book. the names are the actual names of the people presented. Some of them may seem more simple to remember than others. That is because they have been picked to represent a fair cross section of the sort of names and faces you encounter every day. Pictures are more difficult to remember than people in flesh and blood, for you do not have a chance to notice voice, coloring, or varieties of expression. Picture practice is particularly valuable for this reason. If you can remember a group of people by applying our principles to their pictures alone, you will find it twice as easy to remember the men and women you meet in person from now on.

On the opposite page, meet Mr. Voehringer.

MR. VOEHRINGER

Here's a difficult name to remember, probably the most difficult one in the book. See if you can get it the first time. It is spelled V-o-e-h-r-i-n-g-e-r, and it is pronounced *Vo*-ring-er, with the accent on the first syllable. The name rhymes with *adoring her.* Say to yourself, "Mr. Voehringer is adoring her. He is never *boring her.*"

Now, before you go any further, look up at Mr. Voehringer's face. Notice his glasses. Are his eyes light or dark? How does he comb his hair? Notice his mustache and the cleft in his chin. *Fasten Mr. Voehringer's face in your mind.*

Next, study each letter of the name until you can close your eyes and see how it looks. It rhymes with *adoring her,* but it doesn't begin with an *a.* And it rhymes with *boring her,* but it doesn't begin with a *b.* No, the name begins with a *V* It is Voehringer. V-o-e-h-r-i-n-g-e-r.

MR. NEWSOM

You've seen Mr. Newsom before. Doesn't it seem to you that you k*new some*one named Newsom a short while ago? Of course you have—Mr. Newsom's photograph was the first one in this book, illustrating the chapter on Rule One: *Get the Name Right.* Notice Mr. Newsom's steady gaze and firm jaw. He looks like a fellow who knew some people you knew. Good-by, Mr. Newsom.

O. HOWARD WOLFE

I'd like you to meet another friend of mine, O. Howard Wolfe, a prominent Philadelphia banker. Mr. Wolfe is a banker, but he is not the big bad Wolfe. He is O. Howard Wolfe.

Pay particular attention to how he spells his name. Notice that it is spelled with an *e* on the end of it. The name Wolfe can be spelled in a number of ways, but O. Howard Wolfe spells his name with just one *o*, one *l*, and one *f*. One of each, with a final *e*.

But O-how-are you going to remember his first initial and first name? That's right. O-how-are you, Mr. Wolfe? O. Howard Wolfe.

MRS. CARTER GLASS, JR.

If you met Mrs. Carter Glass. Jr., at a party, you would of course think of Carter Glass, the veteran Senator from Virginia, and you might ask her if she were related to him. Yes, Mrs. Carter Glass, Jr., is the daughter-in-law of Senator Carter Glass. This special kind of association would make you remember Mrs. Carter Glass, Jr., in real life, and it will probably enable you to recognize Mrs. Carter Glass, Jr., when you meet her later in this book. As you ponder the association, take a long look at her wavy hair, high forehead, finely arched brows, and light gray eyes, so that you will remember her face as well as you remember her whole name.

MR. FRANK CORTRIGHT

This is **Mr.** Frank Cortright, a Philadelphia real-estate broker. Get his Name Right. If you say to yourself, "Frank Cortright knows his *rights* in *court*," remember to drop the *U* in *court* when you spell his name. It's Frank Cortright. Making a note of his slightly upslanting brows, rather full mouth, and off-center hair parting will help you *Fasten his Face in your Mind*. He is very *frank* when he cortrights. Frank Cortright. Rap the Name in by Repetition. Frank Cortright.

MR. RIPPEY

Study Mr. Rippey's face especially carefully, for more people forget this name than any other in the book. Can you beat the jinx?

Pay attention to the spelling of the name Rippey. Believe it or not, it's not Ripley, with an *L*. It's Rippey, with two *P*'s. Say the name Rippey over and over again until it comes easily. Look at the center part in Mr. Rippey's straight hair. Take notice of his straight nose and protruding lower lip.

We leave you here as you are about to encounter **Mrs. Bryan.**
Remember to scrutinize her face, noting any unusual characteristics of feature or expression, any resemblance to someone else you may know, and Rap the Name in by Repetition.
Do the same with the faces on the pages following. The space
beneath each photograph is left blank so that you may make
any notes that you think will help you recognize it later.

MRS. BRYAN

EDWARD REDFORD

MR. CARSON

MR. HORGAN

Now we will repeat the pictures of these same people, without their names. See how many of them you can identify.

CHAPTER TEN

THE SIMPLE SECRET
OF REMEMBERING PEOPLE
IN GROUPS

"REMEMBER *groups* of people? Never! I consider myself lucky if I can meet two people at once and know their names five minutes later!"

The man who said this to me was the dignified, white-haired chairman of a large industrial firm. And he meant it.

Yet one week later, after he had mastered the principles set forth in this book, that same man was meeting twenty persons at once, and remembering their names with ease. The transformation seemed so miraculous, even to himself, that he said: "I want you to come to Akron and teach my executives how to do the same thing. This is the most remarkable thing in memory education I have ever heard of, and I have been in business half a century!"

Time and time again I have encountered the same attitude—and the same result. Rudolph Stiasny, banquet manager of the Waldorf-Astoria, was equally certain he couldn't remember names. Yet, after he took the course, he was arranging large banquets, meeting dozens of people at once, and addressing each person by name. "I cannot tell you," he said, "how great an advantage this has been. Nothing could have convinced me that I could do this—until I did it. But now I not only remember the names of our customers, but I can remember each person's likes and dislikes. People come back to us again and again, because they can depend on us to remember their individual tastes."

But the mere idea of meeting a number of people at once is terrifying to the average person. So terrifying, in fact, that they don't even attempt to remember names. Failure, they *know*, is a foregone conclusion.

Yet we can remember groups of people, with a little practice, just as easily as we remember one or two, and by applying the very same rules. You can convince yourself of this if you make the experiment at the *very first opportunity*.

GIVE YOURSELF A FAIR ADVANTAGE

My advice to beginners who expect to meet a number of people is: *arrive at the scene early, in order to avoid hurried introductions.*

Ordinarily, people arrive at parties, meetings, and conferences in twos or threes. This means, of course, that if you are on the scene early you can meet them as they come in, and avoid having to run the gamut of a dozen flustered introductions at once.

With this simple precaution. you have merely to observe the same rules we have discussed. You get the name right, you repeat it as often as possible, you analyze the face, and you anchor the name as strongly as possible by association.

There is. however, a second precaution you will find useful in meeting groups: *check yourself as frequently as possible on the people you have already met.* In order to do this, take advantage of any lull in the conversation to glance over the group, repeating the names to yourself. You will obviously find it easier to remember a large group if you stop for this kind of checkup after meeting four or five new faces. If you find that one name eludes you, ask the person sitting nearest you to help you out.

This repeated checkup is really the secret of remembering groups of people. For example, William Donnelly, general superintendent of the Kingsport Press, the biggest textbook publishing house in the world, was recently invited to a dinner party. He decided to try out this method and see if he actually could remember the names of the sixteen other guests present. So he took advantage of those moments when he himself was not engaged in conversation to examine the faces of those he had already met. and repeat the names to himself. When it came time to leave, he had no trouble whatever in calling each person by name as he said good night. And this was all the more remarkable, since he was apparently the only person present who could do such a thing. Nobody else, he noticed, was able to call *him* by name, although they had spent several hours in the same company.

To illustrate the fact that this ability to remember people in groups can be acquired—by practice and by observation of the rules—I myself, on my lecture tours, frequently name one hundred and fifty of the people sitting in the auditorium. I do this, naturally, by asking people their names as they come in the door. Invariably this "stunt" of remembering a hundred people at once is greeted with openmouthed incredulity. Yet, I repeat. it is an accomplishment anyone can master. The secret lies in the four rules we have already studied, plus a frequent pause for a checkup.

NOW YOU'RE READY
TO GO ON YOUR OWN!

HERE ARE TEN new people for you to meet. You are entirely
on your own. Study them as you did the earlier acquaintances,
Getting the Name Right, Rapping the Name in by Repetition,
Fastening the Face in Your Mind, and Anchoring the Name by
Association. You are about to meet:

Mr. Armfield

Mr. Hoen

Dr. Nicholls

Mr. Greentree

Tom Jones

Miss Wortham

Mr. Farley

Mrs. Mitchell

Randolph Dillon

Miss Pilcher

MR. ARMFIELD

MR. HOEN

DR. NICHOLLS

MR. GREENTREE

TOM JONES

MISS WORTHAM

MR. FARLEY

MRS. MITCHELL

RANDOLPH DILLON

MISS PILCHER

CHAPTER TWELVE

ROUND-UP

FINALLY, we present all the people you have met in this book, from Mr. Price, to whom you were introduced first of all, to Miss Pilcher, your latest acquaintance. If you are able to call each one by name you may consider yourself an expert. However, we don't expect a perfect score yet. Though you've come to the end of the book, your training is not yet complete, for your memory will continue to improve for a period of months, as you put this course into practice. Every time that you Rap in a Name by Repetition or Anchor it by Association, you will be helping yourself to a better memory. At this point, you are still conscious of the four rules, but as you go about your affairs, applying them to new faces as they come before you, they will get to be automatic, and before long the names will seem to register *themselves* indelibly in your mind, so little will you be conscious of any effort to remember them.

Good luck to you!

FUN WITH
NAMES AND FACES

OBVIOUSLY, the secret of mastering any system lies in the amount of time that one gives to drill. But drilling oneself may become monotonous unless it can be worked into a social activity, at least occasionally. Fortunately, if you have carefully read and digested and practiced all that has preceded, you are now ready to incorporate in your recreations our system of remembering names and faces. And some group memory contests can be great sport. Have you ever played Name Masquerade, for instance? It is quite simple. Each player assumes a name, and calls it off in his turn, thus: "I am Mr. Langley," or whatever name is chosen. Paper and pencils are distributed, and each player is required to write down the alias of each of the other contestants.

Another game can be played with cut-outs from the roto section. A set of pictures, with the name of the subject marked on each, is passed, one by one, from player to player. After ten or fifteen minutes have elapsed, the hostess holds up the pictures, one by one, and the guests are required to identify them in writing.

Either game can be played with a favor for the winner.

Printed in the United States
67282LVS00011B/65